The Ark of Ukraine

The Ark of Ukraine:
Bringing the Kingdom to a War-Torn Country

Lura Hunter

Printed in the United States of America.

For more information, or to book an event, contact Lura Hunter:

lurahunter@gmail.com

https:/ /www.lurahunter.com/

Editing by Speak Fire Publishing

Published by King's Glory Publishing House (Scribal Champions LLC)

Book design by Desiree T. Young

Cover design by getcovers.com

ISBN – Paperback: 979-8-9910631-0-4

ISBN – Ebook: 979-8-9910631-1-1

First Edition: August 2024

Dedication

This book is dedicated to Irina and Peter Tkachuk, who dared to believe God.

And to Al and Georgine Yeatts, who believed in Peter and Irina.

Lura, Al and Georgine Yeatts

Peter and Irina Tkachuk

Contents

Praise for The Ark of Ukraine

"*Learn to fall in love with a people many miles away, as you experience God's love through the lens that Lura perfectly paints. Discover the victories and tragedies of giving yourself 100% to the calling of God on your life and discovering the fullness of joy as you walk in the calling. The Ark of Ukraine, is set as the story of Noah's Ark Mission, but it is so much more than that. It beautifully showcases the impact that one can have when they fully say "yes" to God. Not only did I discover a passion for the mission of Noah's Ark, it refreshed the passion and calling in my own life. A great book for those who want to be encouraged, challenged and reignited in their walk with the Lord.*"

-Matthew Oliver, Senior Pastor at The Family Church Roseville

"*I really enjoyed the book on the Tkachuk's life of faith in Christ. Anyone who enjoys hearing about saints who are Spirit Filled and sensitive to our Lord's leading will be inspired by the incredible stories contained there in. Moreover, the reader will be challenged to follow suit and surrender their life more completely to Christ. This is a modern day journey of epic scale demonstrating how God's humble servants (the Tkachuk's) experience God's miracles and answered prayer. Read this book and prepare to be blessed.*"

-Pastor Dann Bryant, Retired Missions Pastor at Arcade Church

A Quick Request

If this story inspires or encourages you, please leave a review.

If you grabbed the ebook version of this book, I encourage you to grab the paperback version: **https://a.co/d/0ftruP1h**

Introduction

I had a "light bulb" moment during a board meeting of Noah's Ark Missions, Ukraine. I am a member, and Irina Tkachuk was at the meeting at the time. She was answering the many questions a new board member had about the mission of Noah's Ark. I was annoyed by her many questions and wanted to get on with the meeting. However, I've learned from my life experiences that irritation leads to revelation when examined. So, when I asked God why I was so irritated, He gave me a revelation. When it hit me, a surge of energy rushed into my body, and I realized that the story of this mission had never been told!

Who would tell it?

Could it be that God was asking me to do it? I argued with God about this for a while.

I told my Lord, "I am unqualified! I don't have a "Type A" personality that gets things done! It's too hard! I don't know how!"

There were so many reasons I felt that I shouldn't be the one to be writing this book. But there was one compelling reason I wrote this book—it needed to be written. The miraculous stories, the countless lives that have been touched, the courage, the faith, the obedience of the ministers of the gospel—*all* these stories needed to be told.

Another reason I wrote this book was because I became convinced that *God wanted me to*. I have enough faith to believe that what God calls me to, He will equip me with whatever I need to accomplish it. I knew I could partner with Jesus and the Holy Spirit, and they would not let me be a worker ashamed.[1]

Upon further reflection, I think it is fitting that I, an unknown and unpublished author, should be the one telling the story. The story of Noah's Ark Mission Ukraine is a faith story, a miracle story, a story of the power and the love of God. This story will not be told by me without faith.

My prayer is that the story I tell will build your faith, help you believe in miracles for your own life, and that you would experience the power and the love of God for yourself as you walk by faith. My prayer is that the story my words tell would inspire you to do the good works that God had planned for you from the beginning. I pray you will believe that all things are possible when you partner with God, and you will believe that God will qualify you for what He asks you to do. I pray that you will believe that God will supply all your needs and protect you wherever you go.

When I was planning to travel to Ukraine in 2005 (to help with the children's camps there), I wrote in my journal:

Jeremiah 23:22 But if they had stood in My counsel, then they would have announced My words to My people and would have turned them back from their evil way and from the evil of their deeds.

Father, let me stand in your council, let me speak your words in Ukraine. I pray that you will be glorified. Thank you that you are near, that you will be found by those who do not call on you. Spread your fame throughout the world.

Writing this book is part of that prayer being answered.

***

A bit about myself. I am a retired speech therapist and special educator. I was born in Bieber, a little-known town in northern California. The town is now famous because of the name Justin Bieber, and Instagram folks will snap photos of themselves next to the city sign.

After attending high school there, I went on to college, had a family, got divorced, and then met Jesus. He totally changed my life. He led me to Arcade Baptist Church and there I began my journey of gaining wisdom and knowledge of God. My sister-in-law, Sharon Holl, a believer in Jesus herself, informed me that I should read one missionary book a month, so that was what I began to do. Fortunately, the church had a well-stocked library containing many such stories. This began my love of missions.

It was my absolute joy to be able to go on several missionary trips after my children were grown and on their own journeys. I went to various countries, loving the lifestyle of traveling with fellow believers, of praying together, worshipping together and sharing the stories of what God had done at the conclusion of each day. I loved not knowing what would happen each day. Walking with God became an exciting adventure during those trips.

Two of those adventures occurred in Ukraine.

I went on two trips to Ukraine to help with the children's camps put on by Noah's Ark Missions. The first one was in June of 2005, where I helped with two camps, and the second was in June of 2007, doing the same. These trips made me fall in love with Irina and Peter Tkachuk. They are unique and wonderful people who have, through their faith, been able to accomplish more than they could ask for or imagine!

In this book you will meet them and learn to love them too.

Enjoy your adventure on the Ark!

[1] 2 Timothy 2:15

Chapter 1: Made from God's Blueprint

No life is more secure than a life surrendered to God. –D.L. Moody
Whether you turn to the right or to the left, your ears will hear a voice behind you, saying, "This is the way; Walk in it."
–Isaiah 30:21 (NIV)

Noah's Ark Missions was birthed out of the yielded hearts of Peter and Irina Tkachuk.

A seed was planted in Peter at an altar in a church in Ukraine. It was there that Peter said to God, "Use me and whatever I am." Peter was not a pastor, nor had he gone to the Bible school. But he was willing to be like that little boy in the story of the feeding of 5,000[1] found in the gospels. The boy gave Jesus what was in his hand, five loaves and two fish. With that, Jesus multiplied it to feed over 5,000 people with 12 baskets of fish and bread left over. God took what Peter had: his love for God and others, his love of sports and adventure, his ability to build and work with his hands, and God multiplied it.

[1] Matthew 14:13-21

Peter Tkachuk

We have become his poetry, a recreated people that will fulfill the destiny he has given each of us, for we are joined to Jesus, the anointed one. Even before we were born, God planned in advance our destiny and the good works we would do to fulfill it!

  –Ephesians 2:10 TPT

Peter was born in Slobodysche, Ukraine, on July 12, 1967, to his parents Anna, and Anton. Peter's father had another son by his first wife. She died in childbirth along with their second child. From the union of Anton and Anna, Peter was the seventh child of nine children; of which only two are girls. Peter's father was an orthodox Christian but didn't visit the church often. He passed in 2013. On the other hand, Peter's mother, Anna, was raised in the Christian faith and was strong in her faith. She lived her faith to the point that some of his brothers have started helping with the Noah's Ark ministry since the war with Russia started.

Peter describes his childhood as being a happy one. Raised away from the city, he enjoyed all the freedom and beauty of living in the country. He enjoyed fishing and playing with his friends in the wild. Once he was old enough, Peter got a motorbike and fixed it up. Once he did, he went everywhere on it. Peter was drawn to the adventure of exploration. He and his friends would ride to new places, camp under the stars, then rise the next day to conquer another horizon. This sense of wonder is ignited when he visits other countries even today; always wondering about the people and the places he visits.

Peter remembers going to a small church during his formative years. The congregation consisted of older women and men, but no children attended. His mother, Anna, was a very committed believer. She was always reading her Bible, singing hymns, and speaking about God. She had a very close relationship with Jesus. Peter remembers an early awareness of God. It seemed to him as if he always had this connection.

"I feel God in every thought, in every place, in church or anywhere. I feel God with me all the time. I don't remember a time when I felt separated from Him. It seems like it was this way since birth. He has his eye on me!"

Peter remembers a time when he was riding his motorbike. He often rode with his helmet on, but sometimes without one. One time, he took a very bad spill from his bike, tumbling over and over on rocky terrain before landing on his back. While he lay, the dark night the stars shone brightly down on him. There was no one around to help him or hear his cries. But in the silence, he looked up at the millions of brilliant stars and was transfixed on a revelation of God. He realized that God had saved him for a purpose; God had a plan for his life. What that purpose was would unfold slowly throughout as the years passed. Although Peter would never say this, it seems to me that he is like Paul when he introduced himself in Colossians 1:1.

My name is Paul and I have been chosen by Jesus Christ to be his apostle, by the calling and the destined purpose of God. (TPT)

Peter could introduce himself in the same way saying, "My name is Peter and I have been chosen by Jesus Christ to be his apostle, by the calling and the destined purpose of God."

An apostle means "one who is sent out." An apostle is the builder of the church and is one of the gifts that Christ gave to the church.[1] "These grace gifts will function until we all attain oneness of faith." Along with calling Peter, God equipped him with the gift of faith which is evidenced by his life story.

At a time when Peter was around the age of 16, he was studying in Vinnytsia. Walking home with a friend after attending an event at a church, his friend asked, "What do you see for your future?"

Peter thought about it but could not see anything specific. He wanted to ride his motorbike, but that was a childish dream, and he knew there was more to life than that. He knew that he wanted to be a good person, but beyond that he could not see. He just wanted

God to grab his hand and lead him like a parent does with a child who needs to be led and guided to make good decisions as they mature. Peter wanted to be taught by God. Peter's heart seemed to have echoed that of David when he penned the words, "Now teach me all about your ways and tell me what to do. Make it clear for me to understand..." (Psalm 27:11a TPT)

That cry could well have been answered from Isaiah 43:10, "You are my servant. You have been chosen to know me, believe in me, and understand that I alone am God."

When attending church, Peter heard the message that he needed to come forward to the altar to confess his sins and to invite Jesus into his heart. This is a teaching in the evangelical church, how to be saved and receive the gift of eternal life. Even though there was no reason to believe that Peter wasn't saved already, Peter wanted to invite Jesus into his heart. He didn't understand everything there was to know about God and His ways, but the people at the church seemed to think that this was necessary. He loved Jesus, so it was an easy thing to do. After inviting Jesus into his heart at the church, he was baptized, welcomed into the family of God, and took his first communion. During this time in the country, baptizing a child before the age of 16 was illegal and parents who allowed this could be jailed, pay a large fine, or have their wages appropriated for a month. The timing of this was not lost on Peter, because it was right before his 18th birthday.

In 1985 Peter, at the age of 18, was inducted into the army for his mandatory two-year service. He had no choice in this; it was the army or jail. He chose the army and was sent to the Russian equivalent of Boot Camp for training. All the men who were in good physical shape were sent to Afghanistan (this was a time during the soviet-Afghan war which took place during 1979-1989. Remember, Ukraine did not receive its independence until 1991).

It came time for the last physical testing to be done to determine the future of each soldier. He was sent to a large government building. There was a center room surrounded by many smaller rooms, and Peter went from one room to another, from one doctor to another. He came to the last room and presented his documents.

After the examiner looked at Peter's documents, he demanded, "What is this!"

Peter had no idea what the examiner was talking about until that man showed him his document. Every space that contained a line for information to be filled in was written in blue ink, except one space near the bottom of the document which was written in red.

"Are you a Baptist?" the examiner asked.

"Yes." Peter confessed.

Upon this confession, Peter was taken to a barracks and told not to leave and that he would be called. All his friends were assigned to a military unit and departed with their commanders, but Peter waited for three days. When he was called, he came into a room of high-ranking military leaders, 20 in all. The room was located in the center of a huge building. The room he entered was called "Lenin's Room." Seated around a long table covered in red cloth several officers awaited him. He was asked, "Do you believe in God?" When he answered in the affirmative, he was told, "God is a lie. Old people are dying that believed that, and God is no more." Peter was told that his future was dead too, if he didn't renounce that he believed in God. He would not have a job and his life would be nothing. "You're young, and you're strong, and you can have a good future. All this about God is false!"

Peter answered, "If God is fake, how come, in other countries, presidents and important people put their hands on the Bible and swear on it?" (Peter admits, "I was young. People usually didn't answer back but were quiet when questioned. These men had the authority to take my life without any repercussions.")

One questioner asked, "Where did you hear about this?"

"On the radio, I think," Peter answered.

He was then told that if he didn't change his answer that he would be taken to a place that is worse than jail; he would be taken to a place where he would be made to talk. After about an hour and a half of questioning, Peter was given a paper, then told to return in a month.

Peter returned home elated! This was the first time he felt God make him brave! Despite not being a very courageous man, he was brave in that room with all those men who had the power to kill him! This was amazing! God could do that!

"I felt like I was running before a train!" Peter later admitted.

After his month was over, Peter returned to the same building. Other soldiers were there being assigned to various military units. Surprisingly, Peter was assigned to a construction unit.

He was put on a train but not told where he was going. He arrived in Moscow, assigned to help finish a government building. Peter felt like a slave with no freedom. He worked, ate, slept, then got up and worked again. This was how things went as Peter worked on that building for one month. After that month, he was approached by his commander who asked him if he would like to learn to be an electrician. Peter agreed and was sent to school for two months.

"I saw God in my life every step I was there in the school, before school, you know, everywhere." Peter reflects.

When he came back from school, his commander asked him if he wanted a good position as a type of electrician supervisor. Peter would have authority over the entire building. As a supervisor, he would stay close by and not have to sleep in the barracks with the others, although he would still take his meals with them. Peter took the job and was given a small home to live in. There he had freedom of movement to roam around Moscow and see the sights.

The supervisor asked Peter one day, "Do you know why we chose you for this position?" Answering his own question, he said it was because Peter was a believer. "You believe in God so we know we can trust you. Others don't work hard and drink, but you take your job seriously and have integrity. You stick with the job and do a good job. We don't have to supervise you because God is your supervisor."

Upon hearing that, Peter remembered, six months prior, he was told he would be sent to a place they assured him he didn't want to go and "they had ways to make him talk!" But now he had the easiest job in the building! That was part of God's purpose and plan. Peter rejoiced!

"You have kept me from being conquered by my enemy; You broke open the way to bring me to freedom, into a beautiful, broad place" (Psalm 31:8). "My heart will not be afraid...I know that you are there for me, so I will not be shaken." (Psalm 27:3 TPT)

After his two years of mandatory service, Peter returned home and began to attend church. There he met his future wife, help mate, friend, and companion—Irina. They found that they were a good match, both with strong faith, good intelligence, practical skills, and a deep love for God, for others and for each other. They married the year after they met, on August 12, 1990.

[1] Ephesians 4:11

Irina Tkachuk

An excellent wife is the crown of her husband... Proverbs 12:4 TPT

He who finds a wife finds what is good and receives favor from the Lord. Proverbs 18:22 TPT

Irina was born into a faith-filled family on 11-13-73 in Vinnytsia, Ukraine. She was third in line of 12 siblings. Her parents, Nadia and Volodymer Yukhimets impacted her faith and the faith of her siblings greatly throughout their lives. They had the privilege of watching the love of God through their parents.

"God was very merciful to our family even though we lived at a very hard time in Ukraine's history. There were 12 children, but God always provided. Our parents never let me or any of my siblings feel any stress or fear. What we did feel was so much love! It was one of the biggest gifts in my life, that I was raised in love.

"I had a happy childhood. My family didn't concentrate on our struggles or financial lack because we were focused on our blessings instead. We never traveled or had anything extra, but my father had the gift of making everything like a holiday for us. My parents always pointed out the miracles that God was doing around us!" Irina explained, "I grew up knowing that God was a miracle-working God!

"I was a third child. My parents had three babies in the space of three years. I saw their sacrifice for us and how stressful it was to take care of three small children, and I did not want to make my parents' life any more difficult, so I did whatever I could to not cause them any worry. I was probably the only child in the family that would rarely ever cry. This concerned my parents, and once I was taken to the doctor to see if anything was wrong with me. They wanted to discover why I didn't cry. I wouldn't cry, even if I had a bleeding wound, because I didn't want my parents to worry. I reasoned that because my parents guarded us from painful things, I would guard them from my pain."

This experience is reflected in the way that she is reluctant to voice her feelings today. "I never had a person to share my problems and thoughts with growing up."

Irina's father, a devoted pastor and missionary, passionately spread the gospel in his local region. He shepherded several churches, ensuring their spiritual growth. Volodymer was a compassionate man and would regularly visit the elderly members of the community. His faith and love for Jesus set him apart from the members of legalistic churches which were typical in Ukraine. People aren't known to reach out to their neighbors in love even if they call themselves Christians, but Volodymer was unwavering in his beliefs and worked tirelessly to share the love of Christ with others, which left a lasting impact. His ceaseless commitment to serving the Lord continued until his passing in 2021 at the age of seventy-five. Unable to recover from the loss of her husband of 52 years, Nadia Yukhimets succumbed to her illness two years later, in January of 2024. Irina and her family still feel a profound loss.

Still, the legacy of faith endures in Irina's family. Under Soviet Rule in Ukraine, Irina's great-great-grandfather and his son were exiled to Siberia for steadfastly refusing to renounce their faith. His wife and daughter moved to Siberia to be close to them. Irina's great uncle endured torture and eventually perished in a Siberian prison. Stalin caused widespread starvation in 1930-33 known as the "Holodomor, a term derived from the Ukrainian words for hunger (holod) and extermination (mor)" or "Great Famine"[1] (Applebaum, A. (2024,3)) This was to eliminate a Ukrainian independence movement. According to Britannica, around at least 5 million perished in Ukraine during this time.[2]

The "Great Purge" or sometimes known as the "Great Terror" occurred in 1937-1938.[3] This dark period in history included a mass execution of thousands of people in Ukraine under Soviet control by Stalin, who was determined to purge his perceived enemies. It was during this time that General Secretary Joseph Stalin consolidated his power of the Communist Party.

To say that the Ukrainian people have suffered greatly under Soviet Rule is an understatement.

But the legacy of faith lives on. Irina's siblings are, as of this writing, serving in some sort of Christian ministry. All her brothers are either deacons or pastors. Her father and all his brothers were pastors. Her grandfather was a pastor as well. Faith has sustained every family member.

Irina met Peter at a church meeting in Ukraine in 1989 after he returned home from serving in the army. They married on August 12, 1990, when Irina was only 16 years old!

"It was not easy being 16 getting married," Irina explains. "For many years I kept everything inside me; I wouldn't talk about it. I have learned to trust my feelings and share them with Peter over the years. But still, if I think he won't understand me, I might not share my thoughts or feelings."

"I prefer to deal with everything quickly. I don't like long phone calls. I like to know what someone wants, what their question is, then I answer it and move on. I don't like having long conversations. Even ceremonies, I can't sit through them without getting anxious. However, when it comes to other people's feelings and experiences, I can listen with compassion. I ask God to give me patience and love for others, especially those who are hurting. I have a desire to be present for people, to show them that I care for them, but I never open my heart to anyone else the way they open their hearts to me. I understand that I should, but I don't know how. I often wonder why others share with me so openly. I may seem brave to you, but inside I feel small."

Anna, her daughter, has observed this ability that Irina has during their many times ministering together in one of their camps. She told me, "It seems that people want to share their problems with [Irina]; they recognize that she is a safe and caring person. Her work, compassion and availability to others never ends until her health is so affected that she must stop for a while to heal. This concerns us greatly."

Irina experiences the struggle many followers of Christ have.

She is extremely sensitive to the needs of others and her heart's desire is to help them in any way she can to relieve them of some of their burdens. Irina has the gift of mercy. It is difficult to turn away from the needs she sees around her and so she answers those needs with all her strength. But Irina also has a close connection with God, so she goes to Him for strengthening. Like an empty vessel, she turns to God to fill her up with the love she needs to pour out on others. Thankfully, Irina is growing in her ability to enter the faith-rest life Hebrews 4 teaches about.

As we enter into God's faith-rest life we cease from our own works, just as God celebrates his finished works and rests in them.

–Hebrews 4:10 TPT.

Being yoked to Jesus, she knows that he will pull the heavy weight of loving others and has experienced that in her life.

[1] "Holodomor." *Encyclopædia Britannica*, Encyclopædia Britannica, inc., 29 Mar. 2024, www.britannica.com/event/Holodomor.

[2] ibid

[3] "Great Purge." *Encyclopædia Britannica*, Encyclopædia Britannica, inc., 6 Mar. 2024, www.britannica.com/event/Great-Purge.

Married life and The Jesus Film

Peter and Irina's married life began in partnering together to share the Good News of Jesus Christ. They were asked by their pastor if they could work with young people. Not content to be just a hearer of the word, Peter and a friend joined a group going out to the surrounding villages to show the "Jesus" Film[1], a film telling the story of Jesus taken from the book of Luke in the Bible. Peter and Irina's father (or others) visited many towns and villages in Ukraine promoting and showing the film. During that time, Peter believes he saw The Jesus Film over 400 times! He has practically memorized the gospel of Luke. People came to watch the film, and this gave the others a chance to speak with them, answer their questions and give them a New Testament, "It is a very interesting story," Peter said, "especially for those who have had no prior knowledge of it."

[1] "The Jesus Film | English | Official Full Movie HD." *YouTube*, Jesus Film Project, 9 Mar. 2020, www.youtube.com/watch?v=-Td05XH0TDg.

Home Bible Study

After that experience, Peter and Irina began to host Bible studies in their homes. Their first study consisted of three teenagers. But then these boys brought friends and family members. This group emerged from observing that many young people around them didn't have a community and didn't know about Jesus.

The Tkachuk's home became an oasis. Young people came, laid their burdens down, drank deeply from God's Word, and were refreshed by the love that surrounded them. They learned the ways of faith and forgiveness. They learned to love and allow themselves to be loved. Laughter, tears, celebration, and food became the staple diet at the Tkachuk's home. They not only studied the Bible, worshipped and prayed, they also went traveling, bike riding, picnicking, and just enjoying each other's company. As these young men and women grew strong in Christ and confident in their friendships, they became anxious to serve. Armed with the wisdom and the knowledge of the Lord, they were full of the love of God, themselves and each other. This group grew to about 40 people ready to be "love in action."

Nadia and an Introduction to Children's Camps

Peter and Irina's first child, Nadia Tkachuk, was born August 8, 1991. One Sunday, Peter went to church alone because Nadia was not well. That Sunday the church heard the testimony of a missionary from Siberia. He shared about the work he was doing there and painted a description of the area with his words. The missionary, speaking to about 1,500 people attending, asked them to imagine God pulling a giant sled full of wicked people. Then the missionary asked if there might be somebody, right there in the church, who would be willing to help pull the sled. He described the heaviness of the sled, and how God wanted their help to pull it.

Peter found himself raising his hand along with five others. The missionary asked them to come forward which threw Peter off. He didn't mind raising his hand, but he didn't want to come forward! But he thought, *I just want to help you, God.* When Peter did come forward the missionary prayed for them. That night he shared with Irina what had happened in the church.

They asked themselves, "What does this mean? What's next?"

What came next was an American family who started camps to teach the Bible and the English language to young people. The young people were looking into the future of an independent Ukraine, and many came to these free camps. Irina's father asked them to prepare the American couple a meal for lunch, which they did.

Delivering them their lunch, Peter and Irina had an opportunity to talk with this American couple, Jim and Sandy, about their mission. Jim asked Peter to be a leader in one of the groups, so there would be one American and one Ukrainian leader in each group. Most of these people came to study English and they were not Christian.

Meanwhile, Irina became a Sunday school teacher for the children in their local church. In this capacity, she was sent for formal training. Irina went to Kiev once or twice a month for a year and brought the idea of starting children's camps back home to Peter. During their next home group gathering, they shared the idea of children's camps with their group. The group became very excited and animated with this idea.

"It was like an idea explosion!" Peter recalls. The group decided that they didn't really need a building or anything fancy; they just needed something fun and interesting.

During one of their gatherings, Peter put forth the idea of having a name for their group. Everyone had a good laugh at the suggested names. Looking around, Peter noticed that one person had very large feet, and another had very small ones. He joked to the group that it be called Noah's Ark because they were such a varied collection of people.

The name stuck.

Chapter 2: The Beginning of Noah's Ark Mission

Be shepherds of God's flock that is under your care, watching over them—not because you must, but because you are willing, as God wants you to be; not pursuing dishonest gain, but eager to serve; not lording it over those entrusted to you, but being examples to the flock. –1Peter 5:2 NIV

Out of this enthusiasm and hunger to share what they themselves received; the first Noah's Ark children's camp was launched to teach children about God. The Bible study group had never done anything like it before and they required a lot of planning. There were 30 people from the group who prepared to launch a day camp. The initial camp was held in July 2001 about 50 miles from their house in a village close to Vinnytsia. The church in this village didn't hold a Sunday school for children, so the team went to support that church and the children of that village.

The group knew there were approximately 70 children in that village, however 230 children showed up!

Word of a children's camp had spread to the other villages nearby. This camp would be a welcome change from their uneventful summer. All the children heard the Good News and many of them began their faith life by becoming born again. Bible study participants were wonderful helpers during the children's camps. Their choices had lasting effects.

Later, as adults, three of the youth from the Tkachuk Bible study group became doctors. Two helpers became pastors, one serving a pastor in the US (in Texas). Some leaders now serve as deacons, while others serve as missionaries. One volunteer from Holland, who came to serve in the children's camps, now comes frequently to help bring in food into Ukraine. Sasha, a former leader, now sends his children to the Noah's Ark camps. All the leaders maintained a positive attitude, no matter what circumstances they faced. They seemed to really love all children who came to the Noah's Ark Camp. Receiving that kind of love and attention was a new experience for many of those children.

On occasion, Peter will meet someone who attended one of these children's camps as an adult. Peter once talked with one man works in the post office Peter frequents. This man—who attended a camp in his youth—remembered the volunteer's names, the lessons and the songs!

This might have been due to the framework the Noah's Ark Camp had put in place. The home Bible study team designed a program that presented the gospel one precept at a time. Each day had a theme that corresponded with a color and a concept. It was adapted from the wordless book, a method of evangelism which is commonly used to explain the gospel. The book contains different colored pages. Each color represents a concept to be explained by the one presenting the book.

- Day 1 was black, and the young campers learned about the deceitfulness of sin.
- Day 2 was red, presenting teachings about the blood of Christ.
- Day 3 was white, representing the power of Jesus' sacrifice that could cleanse them from all their sin.
- Day 4 was green, representing how to grow in fellowship with God and each other.
- Day 5 focused on the celebration and the rewards of the Kingdom of heaven, both in heaven and on earth; with the color gold representing that reality.

Apart from the teaching, there were crafts, sports games and food. This camp lasted the full day, and the young campers were sent home for dinner. But the teens were invited back to visit with camp counselors in the evenings. This was a time when the teens could speak openly and have their questions answered. Throughout the camp experience, the team modeled the character of Christ with their peace, patience, love and kindness.

Each camp was different depending upon the children, the situation in the country, and the type of village they were serving in. Camps for children took place primarily in the villages, but some camps were in cities also. According to the needs of the children the group changed the program. If most children liked sports, the camp leaders would accommodate that interest by changing the program to include more sports. If the children were more musical and liked singing, that camp would be changed to include more music.

Some children really loved doing craft projects, so camp leaders would provide more crafts during their time at camp. The leaders changed the songs presented to more popular songs that the children liked. Because each camp had different team leaders, the strengths and ideas of the team leaders were used to modify the camp program. This kept the camps interesting for both the children in attendance and the camp leaders.

Peter wanted to make sure that the team leaders were ministered to and cared for as well as the young people. He didn't want them to feel worn out or depleted. He wanted to make sure that they enjoyed their time at camp. Peter honored everyone's ideas and feedback and was able to provide occasional team outings to help them develop leadership skills.

There were about 30 Noah's Ark Children's Camps led by the group over the years, from 2001-2022. On average, 150 children attended each one of the camps, with a range of 90 to 200.

Anna and Danial

On March 10, 1996, Anna Tkachuk was born. She was named Anna after her grandmother. Then, on July 24, 2002, Peter and Irina added a son to their family. Danial was born, adding joy and delight to their now completed family! Irina prayed that Danial would wait until she had finished preparing for the children's camp before he sent her into labor. He was born during the second day of the camp. Peter had to wait three days to meet him!

Arriving in the US.

Trust in the Lord with all your heart and lean not on your own understanding; in all your ways submit to him, and he will make your paths straight. –Proverbs 3:5-6 NIV

On December 8, 2003, the Tkachuks moved to the United States. They had family members in the US that offered to sponsor them.[1] Peter and Irina ignored the invitation and never took up the offer to come to America. The third letter came saying that this would be the last opportunity for them. At this point, even if a different relative invited them, they would not be welcome into the US. This was their last chance of immigrating to the US.

Peter and Irina decided to accept that invitation, reasoning that it might be an invitation from God. Maybe God was giving them this opportunity; maybe He had a plan for them in this. So, they completed the process and shortly after arrived in Sacramento, California.

"And this was our life," declared Anna.

Moving to the US wasn't something they had ever planned. It almost seemed accidental to Anna. "One day we took a train to Moscow, visiting the American embassy to secure our passports and visa. We knew we had the opportunity to go. And then a couple of months later, we left.

"In 2003, I was seven. That's when we moved, so we moved to the US when I was in second grade. We lived six months in the US, then the next six months in Ukraine."

Peter and Irina would work in the US in the winter, Peter doing construction and Irina cleaning houses while going to college. That was how they earned funds to run children's camps in the summers. It was a huge sacrifice for the whole family.

[1] "Applying for a family-based immigrant visa is the first step in the

process for the person you are sponsoring to become a permanent resident."

"Family-Based Immigrant Visas and Sponsoring a Relative." USAGov, www.usa.gov/sponsor-family-member. Accessed 27 Apr. 2024.

Anna's Story

Anna loved growing up in a house filled with people all the time. For her, her parent's ministry, their love for God, their activities... it all seemed normal to Anna. Only now as an adult, when Anna explains to someone that her parents are missionaries, does it cause her to realize that her life was, in fact, unique. Anna remarked, "I love [my parents'] faith and how they never waited for the perfect opportunity to begin working on whatever God was calling for them to do." When Peter and Irina prayed, when they saw a need or a door open, they would seize the opportunity right then. They went after all the chances that presented themselves. When beginning a project, they would never wait until they had enough finances, or wait for the right weather, or wait for the right year. They would step out in faith and God would provide, every time.

For example, Anna explains, "When they were in the US, the church they were attending encouraged them to go through a big mission organization to start children's camps in Ukraine. [My mom and dad] started the process of working with the mission organization. But that organization told them they couldn't go back to Ukraine until they had a set amount for their support. The mission's organization required that they receive support of about $10,000 a year for their family, and then thousands more for the ministry. They were required to have sufficient financial support established for a couple years before being released back to Ukraine to start the camps for children. This is not the way for Peter and Irina." If her parents had $3,000, but they needed supplies for a camp, they would use their money and trust that God would provide for them later. Which He did. "It has always been like that," says Anna. It was the way her family lived.

But this way of living was hard for the family, especially for Irina. Being a typical mother, she wanted stability and comfort for her children. There were so many times when they didn't know how they were going to get gas, or supplies. But, as Anna stated, "We know God as our backup. He has provided for sure."

Anna explains further how this way of faith living affected her mother.

"I know Mom has had a bigger struggle with that than my dad. He has more of a, 'Let's do it' attitude. My mom, she will do it, but emotionally she will have a harder time." Anna explains. When she, her sister and brother were living in the US, Peter would leave for work when it was dark outside, while she and her siblings were all sleeping. They might just hear him in the morning making lunch for work.

There were times when a babysitter would pick the children up in the morning and drive them to school, and after school Peter would pick them up. Sometimes Anna's mom was able to pick them up, but by then it was "super late and super dark outside." This was their life. They lived through months where the children wouldn't even get to see their parents for long periods of time. Anna's mom, Irina, was cleaning houses while she studied in college as a full-time student until she earned an accounting degree.

Airports were a huge thing in the lives of the Tkachuk family. When Anna was in her early teens, she would say that the airport was another house they had because they were in airports so much. "Some people get stressed flying, but this is something really normal for me," says Anna. "It was just a big adventure which I loved. I mean, I never had a problem flying. I for sure knew that I wanted to live a life like this, it was never boring! I don't know a different way. I mean, yes, there were things I didn't get in life that I had always wanted as a child. I wanted to take piano lessons or dance lessons, but we didn't have the opportunity for that." Anna wanted to do the things that her friends were doing. But that's not what Anna remembers the most. She remembers all the other things; all the adventures she had. "God put in me a kind of a sense of adventure where change was not so hard. It was easy for me. If you told me you got me tickets for Ukraine right now, and that I would have to leave in two days,

I'd be happy to do that. I don't have a problem with doing something quickly. I don't get stressed."

(Interestingly, two weeks after this interview on May 2, 2023, Anna's husband purchased tickets to Ukraine for Anna and their two children. So, 13 days after the purchase of the tickets, on May 17, 2023, Anna left for Ukraine to help with the women's camps.)

Nadia's Story

This lifestyle of faith and hard work and sacrifice was harder for Nadia, the eldest child. As a teenager, she hated moving to Ukraine for three months then moving to the US for three months. Three months here, three months there was stressful for her. Peter and Irina's children attended school in Ukraine then finished the school year in America, or vice versa. Nadia attended and helped with the camps, but she informed her mother that she would not be involved in the camps as an adult. She had her own plans!

You know God laughs when He hears about our plans!

Nadia married Sergy Plysniuk in 2011. They were living in the US at the time. Nadia accompanied Sergy on his long trips across the US as a truck driver, and they enjoyed each other's company. For many years they tried to have children, to no avail. But after many years of disappointment, a miracle happened, and Nadia conceived!

They are being blessed with a boy due on May 20, 2024! Everyone in the family is so excited and can't wait to meet this little one.

After the war began on February 24, 2022, Nadia started helping Irina with the camps, taking food into Ukraine, and in every aspect of the mission. She found herself involved in the activities at the camp and now, she cannot think of anything better. Nadia has a gift of administration and organization which is so needed at the camp. She is also very close to her mother; they enjoy a deep connection which blesses the mission and the family.

Danial's Story

Danial started second grade in Ukraine at age seven and finished that year in the US. "Danial's grammar," according to his sister Anna, "in Ukrainian language or English is bad just because he was always switching languages. His speech is a mixture of English and Ukrainian.." But that didn't hinder him in any way. In the US, Danial liked playing football as a teenager; now he plays for a professional team in Ukraine.

Danial went to Ukraine with his parents when the war started. As of this writing, he is there. Danial was helpful in many ways during the camps and during worship meetings as a drummer. He learned construction as he worked for Max Kusch in the US, so now he builds anything his father asks him to (and usually with a good attitude). In Ukraine, Danial drives a truck to pick up food that had been donated by the Mennonites or sent in from Poland. He helps whenever they need a driver, even driving goods into dangerous places near the eastern border. That's where the team frequently delivers humanitarian aid. When Danial is not doing these things, he supports himself with a job using his computer skills.

Have I Heard You Rightly?

Part of the faith life, at times, is wondering if you have heard God correctly. Peter and Irina began to wonder if all their efforts in organizing, preparing and holding children's camps was worth it. They wondered if they shouldn't put their efforts elsewhere, or if there was any fruit for all their efforts. They had no feedback from any of the hundreds of campers they had fed spiritual food to.

They had become discouraged and needed a word from the Lord.

This time of contemplation came at a time when they were living in Ukraine for several months of the year, then returning to the US to work and save money to fund the children's camps for the following summer. The travel expenses were daunting, and traveling with children was not ideal. It was just a really hard time. Was it worth it?

This was how God answered them.

The Noah's Ark team was planning to return to a village where they held a camp seven years prior. This was one of three camps they were planning that summer. The team met with teenagers in the evenings as they usually did. During one of those evening meetings, four adult women approached Peter and Irina. The women began questioning Peter, asking him if they held a camp at this same place seven years ago. After a brief discussion, they all realized that these women had attended that previous camp! Their conversation revealed that all four of the women were faithful followers of Jesus. They all attended church, and all had been baptized. Their faith was an important part of their lives.

This conversation was enough to convince Peter and Irina to continue the work.

They laid their worries aside. Yes, they had heard God correctly, and were fulfilling their purpose. They praised God, who always answers the cry of their hearts. God also encouraged them with the testimony of a girl, Yana, who became a believer during one of the children's camps. Yana began attending a church in Vinnytsia where she was baptized. She grew up, got married, and is now a leader in a children's church. Now, she faithfully comes and helps with children's camps.

Watching the spiritual growth in those who attend their home Bible studies, delighted Peter and Irina, and even now brings them joy! Members of that group would often invite a friend who would then come to know God and go on to serve in the Noah's Ark camps. There were many stories of those who developed a close relationship with God and whose lives were transformed by Him. Many, many people came through their house and left with knowledge of the Bible, and increased faith, hope, and love. Of those, many have started small Bible groups in their own homes, and many serve in the children's camps which their children now attend.

Then I heard the voice of the Lord saying, "Whom shall I send? And who will go for us?"

And I said, "Here am I, send me!" –Isaiah 6:8 NIV

Chapter 3: My Visit to the Ark

All your children shall be taught by the Lord, and great will be their peace. –Isaiah 54:13 NIV

Jesus said, "Let the little children come to me and do not hinder them, for the kingdom of heaven belongs to such as these." –Matthew 19:14 NIV

I have no greater joy than to hear that my children are walking in the truth. –3 John 1:4 NIV

My Trips to Ukraine and Noah's Ark

Children are the future of any nation. As was mentioned earlier, Peter and Irina felt an urgency to bring the message of Jesus Christ to the people of Ukraine. Conducting camps for children was one of their first ambitions and seeing the world through mission trips was mine.

I was blessed to be able to travel to Ukraine twice to help with these camps. My first trip was in June 2005, where I helped during two camps held in Polohy, Ukraine and a nearby village. This was the hometown of Max Kushch. Our team from the United States consisted of Al and Georgene Yeatts, Lilia and Max Kushch and their two boys, and Peter and Irina and their three children, Linda Edmonson, and me. Linda and I were to help Georgene with the crafts she had prepared in the US. Well, I did help some, and came with her. We would be joining about 20 Ukrainian young people who will be camp leaders.

Linda Edmondson, a dear friend of Georgine and a supporter of the mission, became my traveling and ministry partner. We arrived safely, after many hours of travel, in Vinnytsia. This was Linda's first mission trip; she was so excited to partner with what God was doing in Ukraine, as was I!

While we Americans waited to leave for Polohy, Ukraine team, under Irina's direction, gathered the food and the supplies. Irina organized the team that would be working with the children at the camps. Several of us went on a sightseeing tour around Kiev and viewed the oldest building, St Andrew's Church, built in 1747. Hitler used it as a hide out, and it is said to be built over catacombs, or so we heard. We also learned of a famous surgeon, Nikolay Pirogov, 1810-1881, who entered medical school at the age of 12 and was a surgeon by age 21. He founded the Red Cross in Ukraine and even designed tools for surgery. Dr. Pirogov, known for field surgery as well, was the first to use ether during surgery and to put on casts for broken bones.

There was so much history in Kiev!

Irina's father and grandfather are currently preachers and evangelists who have always been bold, taking every opportunity to preach the gospel. After our sightseeing, we picked up some New Testament books and joined a boat tour. Irina's dad pointed out the place on the river where Christians went to get baptized at night during Soviet Rule. The people being baptized were often shot at or stoned. After some time on the boat ride, the music was turned off and Irina's dad preached the gospel over the loudspeaker. The people on the boat all sang a song, then Irina's father and grandfather handed out New Testament books to the passengers.

We were so impressed with his zeal and with the kind reception he got from the passengers. I silently wondered what would happen in the US if we did something like that.

The First Camp – June 26, 2005

Train travel was quite an adventure! At the train station. It was not clear which car we were supposed to go into. We ran up and down the platform, looking for a certain car number. We were told that indicated the train car we were to embark on. We only had five minutes to get on the train! There were different places where numbers appeared on the train cars, so I didn't even know where to look. I was of no help whatsoever. We finally located the car, and goods were thrown into it quickly. Irina had gathered mountains of supplies for the trip and the camp. By the time we found our car and got the supplies on the train, we had to quickly crawl over them or get left behind. It turned out to be great fun, only because we made it on board!

We were assigned two sleeping rooms in one car, but I was supposed to sleep in a room with a very angry man who didn't want to share his space with me.

My feelings exactly!

I stayed and visited with others on the trip in Al and Georgine's room until I could avoid it no longer. Everyone needed their sleep. I crept quietly into the room and climbed into the upper bunk. After restless sleep, I left the room and headed toward the bathroom. Fortunately, I met Al coming back from the bathroom and he invited me to sleep in the top bunk of their room!

Relief!

Al assured me it was okay, even though I would be interposing on their 50th wedding anniversary. After an all-night train ride, the team arrived at Polohy with the mountain of supplies. We joined a celebration in the town square which I never discovered the purpose of. There was a statue of Lennon that seemed to loom over the town square. I thought it strange that they hadn't removed him.

But I went on and enjoyed the celebration and passed out invitations to the camp which would start the next day, a Monday.

Linda and I stayed with a local family as there were no hotels in town. Tanya and Sasha were our hosts along with their daughters, Anna and Tisha. No one spoke English. Tanya's mother was very frail and had a bad heart. When Tanya was four, her mother, being a Christian, had a very hard life. She almost lost her children because the government threatened to take them away. Tanya and her sister were the only Christians in the school, and they were ridiculed by their teachers. The children were told that they would never marry or find a job and that they were stupid. They were even made to sit at the back of the class.

Teachers often stood in the doorways of the church to stop the children from entering, but her mother didn't listen. Tanya was given an unfavorable report by her teacher which almost stopped her further education. She needed the teacher's recommendation to enter school to become a nurse. But by the grace of God, she was admitted and able to obtain a nursing degree.

There is nothing that God cannot do!

When we weren't at Tanya and Sasha's house or working at the camp, Linda and I enjoyed walking around the neighborhood where the camp was held. I noticed many flourishing gardens filled with vegetables and flowers. Some houses had the window lentils painted bright blue. Loving flowers and gardens myself, I felt like I was in my happy place! While I was walking around, looking and taking pictures of all the flowers, there was a car of men who were suspicious about me. They observed as I took pictures of houses and later talked to the leaders at camp about it.

The local authorities also removed a small crumbling building on the school site within the town. The camp was held on the school grounds, including the front steps of the school. Apparently, they were concerned about what sort of propaganda we would be releasing in the press back in the US. I thought it was curious.

The camp took place while the school was closed on break. Fortunately, we were able to use the kitchen inside the school to prepare meals. It was standard practice to offer some bit of food in the morning and a full lunch in the afternoon. Since there was no indoor plumbing, we all used an outhouse (indoor plumbing was not standard in small towns and villages).

We were as ready as we could be.

The numbers of children who arrived and participated in the camp changed daily. On Monday, the first day, there were 40 children registered. Tuesday, there were over 100 children. 25 orphans were added to the camp on Wednesday. By Thursday, there were 200 children in attendance. Some older boys came only to watch, and later, they were invited to come in the afternoon and talk with the counselors, which they did.

We Americans, Georgene, Linda, and I, along with a bilingual Ukrainian girl, Julia, oversaw the crafts. Each day, the children cycled through in groups with their group leader. We had them make something different each day: a small picture frame they decorated, a doorknob hanger, a beaded bracelet with wordless book colors, an origami snake, a bandana they painted. The children were happy to create and took their projects home with them.

On the steps of the school, an ark was made, consisting of black plastic sheeting on a wooden frame. It was quite clever and fun. The camp began with an opening song along using hand motions, then the children went with their counselor to hear a lesson. After that was sports, then they created crafts. Each child was also given a simple meal. At the end of the camp the counselors reported that about 20 children confessed Christ as their savior.

Praise the Lord!

All the children who attended the camp, including the teens, had heard the gospel, and most of them for the first time. Alex, the pastor who had committed to pastor these new believers, collected their contacts numbers and addresses. He planned to follow up with them and their families.

On Friday, the last day of the camp, they had "water day" and the counselors made a "slip n' slide" with plastic, water, and lots of soap. The children all absolutely loved that activity. Exciting plans were made for Friday night, to conclude the event. The men found a lot of wood and stacked it high while the children invited their parents for the finale—a bonfire lit in the evening. Songs and laughter filled the air.

It was a great celebration!

The Second Camp – July 2005

The second camp occurred a few days later at a school in Tarasovka, which was built in 1962.

There were more difficulties there. The water, drawn from a well, was undrinkable. We had to provide all the children with bottled water. The cafeteria, too far away to walk to, required busing the children there and back. Many camp leaders became sick, but they carried on. Wednesday of that week was windy, cold, and snowing, and the children had to be moved indoors. But even with these difficulties, the leaders taught their classes and prepared fun activities for the attending little ones, and more children arrived daily as the children invited their friends.

Several children came from Polohy from the first camp, and so several of us got a ride with them. Linda and I "prayer walked"[1] the area while the children were in their groups being taught by their team leader. We also prayed for the young man who ran away from his foster home. He seemed to understand the teaching and accepted the gospel during camp.

Not everyone was welcoming. An angry mother came and took her son out of camp. But that was a rare occurrence. About 150 children attended that second camp and about 60 teenagers come in the evening to talk. 70% of them had never heard the gospel before. We showed The Jesus Film in the evening. After a short time, leaders noticed changed lives among the children. They stopped cursing, drinking and smoking. There was a soldier, a friend of some of the teens, came to find out why this was so. The children said they felt peace when they entered the school grounds.

Jesus, the Prince of Peace, welcomed them.

During the evening meeting, the gospel was presented in several ways. Each group got up and presented their "program" for the camp. They each invented a name, a motto and a song. Pasha, a team member, presented a pictorial story of the Titanic and wove in a gospel message. Max then got up and preached the gospel in his way. At his invitation, two young men came forward to indicate that they were giving their lives to the Lord. There was a pantomime skit done to music about how God created man and about the fall of man into sin. After several skits, Alex preached and gave an invitation for anyone who wanted to give their lives to Jesus. Almost all the children ran up to receive Jesus Christ as their Lord and Savior.

What a time of joy and celebration!

After this children's camp concluded, youth camps started. Five of the new believers attended the youth camp in the mountains. Following this camp, a children's club on Sunday afternoon was attended by 13 children. Linda and I returned to the US, but the work of the Noah's Ark team continued.

[1] Prayer walking is a type of intercessory prayer that involves walking to or near a particular place while praying. As you prayer walk, your prayers extend beyond your own concerns, focusing directly on the needs of others and opening yourself to see them with God's eyes and heart. From:

"The Prayer Walk." C.S. *Lewis Institute*, 8 June 2022, www.cslewisinstitute.org/resources/the-prayer-walk/.

Noah's Ark Children's camp in Solbodesia

I had the privilege of visiting Ukraine a second time in 2007, to help with the children's camps in Slobodskaya. This was in the same region where Peter and Irina were married. This region held significance as it was Peter's childhood home where his parents resided. The camp took place in a cultural center, which was originally established by the Communist Party to indoctrinate people to their way of thinking. Interestingly, I observed that the children in this area seemed more trusting compared to those in the eastern regions. Many of them appeared more receptive to the gospel.

After a terribly long flight, I arrived in Ukraine with luggage. My suitcases and I were collected then deposited in a very comfortable spot. For this trip, I stayed in Vinnytsia, in an Operation Mobilization mission house. It was lovely, and not far from Peter and Irina's house. A very generous young woman there gave up her room for me to sleep in. There were many interesting people to visit with there from various countries and I was so glad that most could speak English. I made new friends while Irina was very busy gathering and organizing piles of supplies needed for the camp at their home. It was amazing to see all the supplies piled up around their house.

When the time arrived for us to travel to the camp site, miraculously, everything was loaded on a small bus. Then the camp counselors and I squeezed in and road to the camp surrounded by supplies. What joy it was being together, singing songs and sharing whatever I could without knowing Ukrainian. I shared my iPod with one of the counselors and was happy that music will always be a shared language.

During our visit, we attended church established the previous year. It was the first church service following a Noah's Ark Camp.

The church acquired a building that was half of a house. Additionally, the church had three animal pens, a small barn, and a field extending from the back of the house. The church women generously contributed their labor to the fields by planting, weeding, and harvesting. That work helped support the pastor. It was remarkable to witness how a children's camp could lead to the birth of a new church, but this became a pattern that occurred frequently.

Georgene and I prayer walked around the school and the cultural center, then found a tree in the shade by a pond complete with fisherman, geese, and ducks. We had a sweet time worshipping God and enjoying His presence.

I admit, at times, that I felt a distance from God. But He never left me.

One day I was feeling a little blue and I sat on a windowsill in the schoolhouse and wondered why I was there and if it really mattered. Just then the clouds parted, and the sun came out. The warm light on my face was like a kiss from God! All my doubts vanished right then.

This may seem strange to any reader, but the fact is, God speaks to us in a myriad of ways. Because of my history and experience with God, I knew it was His way of saying, "I'm here. I'm with you." God speaks to us all the time, but we don't always perceive it. The book of Romans talks about how God speaks to us from nature, including from the wisdom of times and seasons. As a person begins to understand this about God, they will hear Him more and more clearly.

God speaks to each of us in a language that we can understand.

An Important Lesson

After the first day of camp, I led a prayer encounter with the counselors. A prayer encounter consists of singing, reading scripture and praising and thanking God. Everyone participates as led by the Holy spirit. After a time of reading scripture, praying and singing, we gathered around the table and took communion together. I modeled the elements by the experiences I had during the prayer encounters I had participated in myself to prepare the communion table. I didn't realize that some people would be hesitant to take communion without it being given by a priest or pastor. But I relied on Peter to calm their fears and explain why it was okay. I forgot how religious and afraid believers can be and I hadn't anticipated this. I was abusing my new-found freedom, and unintentionally causing a stumbling block for others!

It was only later that I realized that I needed to ask more questions about the culture and expectations of those I would be leading before assuming I knew already. I recommend learning about a country and its culture, including religious culture, before taking any lead in ministry. Ask *many* questions and assume nothing! Unfortunately, I caused some problems for Peter, but he was able to calm their fears and explain the freedom that we have in worship.

Fortunately, I've gained wisdom and spiritual maturity over the years. I've learned more about my biases and assumptions. They are often revealed in different cultures when I am confronted with completely new ways of seeing things. I have learned to develop cultural sensitivity over the different missions trips I have been on.

Three of the books that have helped me with this are:

- *Misreading Scripture with Western Eyes: Removing Cultural Blinder to Understanding the Bible* by E. Randolph Richards and Brandon J. O'Brien

- Cross-Cultural Servanthood by Duane Elmer, and
- African Friends and Money Matters: Observations from Africa Second Edition by David E Maranz.

There are many more helpful books that can help one be more prepared to understand and to serve different cultures. I would recommend investigating before going.

For this trip, my camp partner was Al Yeatts. We presented cultural lessons and a variety of other messages. The children shared their culture and traditions, and Al and I taught about the US holiday called Independence Day on July 4th. We also [1]taught them to sign the song "Jesus Loves Me" and did a blind, trust walk. We even taught them the "Hokey-Pokey" song and dance!

Just so you know we were serious about our assignment, in addition to these lighthearted experiences, Al shared a Bible story each day.

During the camp we stayed in a school building. Georgine, such a lovely woman, was my roommate. Someone found some mattresses for us which we put on the floor, and I was happy to get them! The men constructed an outdoor shower for all of us to use as well. It consisted of black plastic surrounding a wooden frame and an old gas tank for the water. The water would sit in the tank all day, then in the evening we would have nice warm water to shower with. Don't worry, the tank had been cleaned out. During the shower, a person could stand on a board on top of two tires. I thought it was quite clever and was happy to have a warm shower to look forward to after a long day with the children.

I encourage everyone to embark on a short-term mission and to experience different cultures. I assure you that God will be your guide! He will surround you with His grace so you can be blessed and so you can bless others.

In the countries that I have been able to go to, the people there will often ask, "Why did you come?" This gives me an opportunity to tell them I had to come to tell them about the best news I've ever heard! I have had the joy of sharing the Good News many times.

The trips I've taken have been the best times in my life and I loved waking up in the morning and wondering what God was going to do that day. I also loved reflecting in the evening about what He had done. Serving others and sharing faith with a group of like-minded people is most delightful! Witnessing to the transformation that God brings in other's lives is pure joy!

[1] "In this variation of the trust fall game, one player, the communicator, guides her blindfolded partner through a maze of obstacles using only verbal directions." From:

Education.com (2012) Trust walk: Activity, *Activity | Education.com*. Available at: https://www.education.com/activity/article/trust-walk/ (Accessed: 04 May 2024).

Chapter 4: Building the Ark

Every house is built by someone, but God is the Designer and Builder of all things. –Hebrews 3:4 TPT

Rafting/Camping Evangelism

Upon receiving a raft for fishing for his birthday, Peter Tkachuk's mind began to imagine all that he could do with rafting.

How could this be used for ministry?

Imagining and sharing what he was thinking with Irina and other team members ignited their imagination as well. Soon a plan was formed, and that plan became a reality. Peter was going to take the team on rafting trips!

Each of the team members were to invite an acquaintance to go on the raft trip in order that they themselves could go. The majority of the team, as well as those invited, had no prior experience with rafting. But that was not going to stop them. Significant planning and preparation went into these trips as they tried to anticipate every need. Shelter, food, dishes, washing dishes, digging a toilet, musical instruments, etc., even a swimsuit code had to be established. The Tkachuks thought about the level of comfort for everyone (If you've ever been on a camping trip, you can easily remember how much preparation is involved).

The rafting expeditions lasted for 7-10 days, consisting of a combination of rafting and camping along the river's route. Two rafts were used to transport essential supplies such as food, sleeping bags and other necessities. Each day was packed with challenges, including navigating through rapids, avoiding rocks, maneuvering through shallow waters, and passing under low bridges. Novice rafters quickly came to appreciate the intensity of the sun after they ignored offerings of sunscreen. They ended up with painful sunburns. But there were many beautiful moments to accompany the harsher lessons.

Throughout the day, rafters enjoyed a continuous supply of sunflower seeds, something people in Ukraine seem to have a continual hunger for. The sunflower is one of the most important crops to the Ukrainian economy, second to wheat production. As we rafted and camped, the surrounding fields were ripe for harvest with abundant grain and sunflower crops waiting to be gathered. It was a beautiful sight!

A few times, the rafters got innovative when frustrated by the slow-moving waters. One time they used a plastic sheet as a sail when the wind was blowing in the right direction. They enjoyed the scenery provided by the fertile soil of the steppe. There were tall trees, green grasses, and wildflowers that grew along the riverbanks. As the team passed through, they were often serenaded by lowing cattle grazing in nearby fields.

During these excursions, no tents had been included among the already heavily laden rafts. Consequently, when it rained unexpectedly, the teams found themselves hastily grabbing tarps to erect lean-tos for shelter. On more than one occasion, they had to rush to safeguard their entire stockpile of equipment from washing away in the downpour. Fortunately, during these challenging moments, one of the team members issued a distress call so friends from a nearby city could come to the rescue. And they did, promptly arriving with trucks and saving the supplies and the day.

Each evening, everyone pitched in to set up camp and prepare dinner. After dinner was praise and worship where the team would talk about the love and the goodness of God. Peter led the campers into their own time of hearing from the Lord. Campers were instructed to spend time alone with God in prayer, inviting a personal encounter with the living God.

Information about God will not bring transformation, but an encounter with God will.

Scripture invites everyone to seek His face. These worship encounters with God and His love (modeled by the example of Peter and his team) brought about transformed lives through each person's own connection with God in the wilderness of the steppe.

In the morning, the team ate breakfast, loaded the rafts, then they were off for another day of adventure together. It was a time of sharing stories and laughter as well as enjoying some serious water fun. The combination of friendship, fun, and times in communion with God brought about lasting changes in their lives. And at the conclusion of each raft trip, new believers were invited to join a study group, anxious to continue their new friendships as well as look deeper into their faith.

Home Bible Study

Peter an Irina held small Bible study groups in their home in Vinnytsia several days a week when they were there. Different people came on different nights. They held a Bible study for men, one for women, and a youth study depending on the day. People would also come over to visit, pray and seek counsel. Even those who were not sure about what they were hearing concerning Jesus were invited and came to learn more. Peter and Irina also hosted local teens every Saturday night to help them grow in faith. Peter and Irina's love and authenticity ignited people's desire to know God and learn how to follow Christ.

After a time, some of the team members began to host studies in their homes as well, following after the model Peter and Irina set. In these studies, the team taught the Bible, and the participants could ask questions without embarrassment. Each Bible study location was a friendly, accepting place and every person was treated with honor and respect. They all formed friendships and bonds with their brothers and sisters in Christ.

The women got together and supported each other in prayer as well. They shared advice concerning their relationships with their husbands and children. In this way, they strengthened one another. This exemplified the admonishment found in 1 Thessalonians 5:11 which asks believers to encourage one another and build each other up.[1]

Over the years, the team found a favorite camping spot along the rafting route, and they returned to that location for the next 12 years. The team cleaned up the grounds by removing dead trees and leveling the grounds for the tents. They also planted over 200 trees and fixed a bridge during their clean up times.

The team would help people that they met near their camping spot. The men would cut wood for widows and the women would clean houses. They became friends with the people who lived nearby and were able to demonstrate the love of God to them whenever they visited. The team even began to use the area for other camping ministries as well.

As will happen when faced repeatedly with various obstacles, camping got more practical. Tarps were put up before it rained, and supplies were brought in by car. This back-breaking work spanned several days and transformed the camping site into a significantly improved (and safer) location. Peter possessed a continuous vision for enhancing things. He consistently formulated plans, enlisted assistance, and turned those plans into tangible realities.

The camps were labor intensive. They had to be set up manually, one camp for adults and one camp for children a short distance away. Two kitchens had to be set up, with toilets dug along with the tarps and tents for 300 people. Afterwards, the entire camp had to be dismantled. All supplies had to be packed into vehicles, taken to Vinnytsia, unpacked, cleaned, organized and stored.

Two weeks later, the Noah's Ark team would prepare for another camp.

Three different camps were offered during the summer months. Unfortunately, in 2017, the last camp on the river was a deal breaker for Peter and Irina. That summer, a storm came through and flooded the river. As the river rose, the first row of tents was in danger of being swallowed! People scrambled to move the tents, but there was no place to move them to. Meanwhile, all the supplies had to be rescued before they floated away.

One family camped under a large tree. A mother, her daughter (who was disabled), and her baby were placed in mortal danger due to the storm. The mother had just moved her baby to a tent in the second row of tents when a tree fell directly onto her tent. Had she not moved her children, they would likely have all been killed!

This incident shook Irina and Peter to the core. They were exhausted with putting on camps in this way, but that kept doing it. However, they could not fathom the thought of putting people in harm's way. They asked God for help and direction because they could not continue the camps as before.

Peter and Irina cried out to God, "We cannot bear it if something happened to one of these people. Our hearts cannot take it!" A short while after returning home, Peter suggested to Irina that they go back to the campsite and pray. Irina could not bear the thought of returning to the campsite. She usually avoided it, as it reminded her of all the hard work involved. But this time she agreed.

She and Peter spent three days at the site praying and seeking God's heart.

One day, as they took a walk toward a village nearby, their eyes were opened to a building they had probably walked past many times before. This time they turned aside and looked.

[1] "Therefore encourage one another and build each other up, just as in fact you are doing."

The Schoolhouse for the Ark

What they saw was an abandoned schoolhouse. They were able to go inside and inspect it. It was red-brick, one story high, and T-shaped. The school, they later found out, had been built in 1905. Having already found peace through prayer, Irina smiled at the possibilities. They inquired about the likelihood of renting the land at the campsite, thus having the ability to construct some permanent fixture on the site. Unfortunately, they were told no by the local government officials. The landowner would neither sell nor rent that land. Then Peter asked about the schoolhouse. The officials told them how many people wanted to buy that property, but unfortunately, the government officials did not have the money or time to prepare the documents necessary to auction off the building. Completing the paperwork could easily take up to three years!

Feeling confident that she could do it, Irina asked if she could prepare the papers. She was given assent but told that she would have to pay all the filing and administrative fees, and after doing all of that, the building would still be auctioned. So, there would be no guarantee that the building would be theirs.

They were not hindered; in fact, they began to imagine what ministries they could do there. Peter and Irina knew they could make a beautiful place there, but in no way had they fully understood what God had in mind. They thought about how much easier it would be to build something permanent for the camps. How easy it would be to hold various camps without having to contend with the rain and floods and the constant setting up and tearing down. They could hold more types of camps and minister to many more people during different times of the year!

Peter and Irina could have never conceived of the difficulties that lie ahead. The obstacles in obtaining this property loomed large in their mind, as well as their visions. How could they do this? What if they were able to do the paperwork and not be able to come up with the highest bid? They had zero money for this!

Peter and Irina dreamed, prayed and worried.

Finally, they reached out to their friends Al and Georgine Yeatts in the US. Al's first reaction was of uncertainty, and he recommended that they pray some more about this. The second call to Al and Georgine signaled their approval! The Yeatts had come to understand that this was what God wanted them to do. All in agreement, they began.

With surety and faith, Irina initiated the great endeavor of completing a mountain of government paperwork! Irina assured me that she would have never taken this on had she known how difficult it would be. She worked on it daily. Many times, it appeared unsurmountable, with no apparent path forward, as if she hit a wall. However, later, she would miraculously see a crack in the door and be able to advance. At the end of the process of readying for the auction, Irina spent time in Kiev daily.

Noah's Ark Ukraine Supporters in the USA

The mission supporters in the United States of America caught the dream and had faith that this was God's plan. They saw what an amazing opportunity the school would be! When God shuts one door, He opens another! Wasn't this just like God to show them a clear direction for ministry just like He had always done? Peter and Irina sent a prayer letter to their supporters dated May 1, 2019. In it they explained the process.

"We know you are waiting to hear about the building and the process of buying it. It has been a lot longer than we expected it to be."

That was an understatement of what they had been faced with. When the directors of the village originally decided to sell the old school building, Peter and Irina were told which documents the directors needed to sell the property, and primarily Irina prepared them. After they completed these documents, they were informed that additional documents needed to be submitted. This was the first time the village directors experienced selling this kind of property/building, so it was all new for them too.

Since it was a government building, it belonged to the country of Ukraine. All the documents needed to first be sent to Kyiv, the capital city, for approval. Next, they had to be approved through Vinnytsia, and lastly, the village would have to approve them also. The documents had to prove that the school was not a historical building, which would prevent it from being sold and remodeled.

"It looks like everything should be ready by August and we can immediately start remodeling," they predicted hopefully.

It did not take Irina three years to prepare the documents, as initially predicted. It took less than one—only 10 months! The documents had been prepared, and the notice that there was to be an auction had been publicized and posted by Irina.

The auction took place on October 18, 2019.

The time had come! After prayer, Peter and Irina put in their highest bid, an amount that was raised by supporters in the US. Then we all held our breath. Surprisingly (or not so surprisingly according to your faith), they won the bid! A whole lot of celebration took place in Ukraine and in the US when everyone found out!

God did it! Peter and Irina did it! Wahoo!

But imagine Irina's shock when she learned that the land around the school had to be purchased! The bid they won was for the building only. What were they going to do without land? Later, they bought the land, grateful to learn that they didn't have to bid on it. They finished paying the bid in November 2019. The following day, they had to fly to the US to complete their citizenship process. Fortunately, they received a large donation from a supporter and friend. Soon after that, they were able to hire a contractor to connect electricity and water to the building while they were gone.

Winning the bid strengthened Peter and Irina's faith that God had given them the Ark, but they knew their gift came with a pick and a hoe. There was so much work to be done in renovations before any of the dreams could come to reality and they progressed one step at a time. Despite the enormity of the task, surety kept them moving in faith toward renovating the school building. Often, Peter and Irina felt the prayers of the team of supporters, which strengthened and encouraged them. In their mission's newsletter dated August 6, 2020, one can get a glimpse of the amount of work that was being done.

In the last month, we were able to clear out a big area of land with the help of many volunteers and a couple of tractors. We were able to set up an outdoor kitchen with running water, a gas stove, washing machine, a septic system and other crucial necessities for temporary living. We plan to completely take off the old roofing, get a big section of the fence done, and clean walls down to the brick on a third of the building by the end of this week. Because we don't have the funds to hire help, Peter has been at the building site this entire month; he hasn't even spent one night at home. Praise God, we have had a lot of volunteers, especially on the weekends, and every Sunday we have held a service together.

It was during this time that they learned how God had been working on their behalf through a man, Sergey. Now, Sergey was the owner of the land adjoining the school property, a believer and follower of Christ, and a Catholic. He put in his papers to get a chance to bid on the old school for himself, planning to start a business there. Sergey had been waiting for someone to complete the paperwork so the property could be auctioned, and he even purchased a plot of land alongside the property where the school sat. However, after he heard about Noah's Ark and the vision that God had given Peter and Irina for the property, he struggled in his conscience about what to do.

During the live auction, with papers prepared, he was ready to bid a high price, one he was sure would secure the building for himself. As he was sitting by his computer, he felt a check. Sergey felt God's hand on his shoulder, and he was sure that God didn't want him to put in his bid. After he decided to let Peter and Irina have the bid, he closed his computer with a sigh of relief, knowing he had done the right thing.

Peter learned of this when he asked Sergey if they could buy a small portion of his land. The land was right behind the school building and Peter wanted to purchase the land even outside the property line. Sergey, with delight, surprised them by offering Peter the whole acre for a much lower price than its value.

With this extra land, the Ark would have enough area for a sports field, a place to set up tents, and whatever else they would add to their vision (as of this writing, Peter and Sergey have become good friends and Sergey accompanies Peter to bring supplies to the east war zone).

They have since learned about two others who were bidding on the school property. One man said that his credit card wouldn't go through, and he couldn't complete his bid, and another man felt strongly that the bid should go to Peter and Irina, so he didn't bid at the last minute.

Interesting, yes?

God amazed Peter and Irina with this confirmation! He was indeed watching out for them. God can do much more than we can ask or imagine! It was this kind of favor which happened repeatedly during the process of renovating the building and clearing the grounds. Their faith and confidence in God continued to be strengthened during these times. Whenever they reflected on what God did for them in the past, when they struggle with doubt about their future, they are strengthened anew by these gentle reminders of the Father's provision.

Not losing sight of the original purpose of the property, Peter and Irina planned two camps for that summer: a women's camp and a men's camp. The renovation continued before and after the camps.

In July, Peter tackled the shoulder high grass around the entrance, helped by volunteers. One weekend, a group of about 30 people came together and much was accomplished with their many hands. They knocked down a few walls and cleaned the plaster off some of the walls, all the way down to the bricks. They worked and sang, praying together, and sharing with one another about what God was teaching them. The joy of the Lord was their strength!

Some of the projects completed before the summer camps included the fence and a new roof. They created an upstairs area, adding another story and completely constructed a new roof to accommodate the changed structure. Electricity was run into the building in time for the first camp. From the beginning of the renovation, continuing forward into 2024, shipping containers have been sent to Ukraine. The containers were packed full of useful items for the ministry, the building, and later for making care packages to give to the people of Ukraine.

The renovation project seemed never-ending, and some days it was overwhelming, but every time Peter and Irina felt discouraged, God reminded them that He has always been with them. He was aware of their needs and would supply all that they needed.

Shortly after one of these down times, a group of men surprised them by helping them raise the second floor. Later that week, they started on the roof. Interestingly, shortly after completing a huge portion of the roof, it started raining. God's timing is perfect!

When they started the building project, they didn't consider the costs, as it was impossible to estimate. The expense of all the materials was incredible! But God was faithful to provide for *every* need at the perfect time.

"We live on grace alone," said Peter. "Every month is different, and we never know what to expect. God provides for our needs. We do not know what to expect, but we are confident that God will provide as He always has." This is the experience of Peter and Irina; it is their reality.

Peter slept in the rear of his van for two years as he worked on the building. Rarely would he return home to Vinnytsia during this time. He was a tireless worker, shedding around 45 pounds throughout the summer of 2020 and seldom indulging in sleep. Meanwhile, Irina remained in the city, deeply engrossed in various activities such as attending meetings regarding the acquisition of citizenship papers. She was also procuring essential supplies for camps and construction, organizing groups, and arranging for the transportation of materials to the construction site. Their list of impending projects before the onset of winter was quite costly. Plumbing, electrical work, cement pouring, flooring installation, roofing, metal sheet roofing, gutter installation, and window fitting were just some of the items on the list. Peter, Irina, and the partners placed their complete trust in divine provision, partnering Gods' provision with their hard work.

By December of 2020, the building was ready for the winter, the grounds around the building had been cleared, the fence was finished, the second story had been added, and the roof was complete. The windows and doors were installed as well. Two large, covered patios had been built on each side of the building, holding a seating capacity of 130 people each. One side was set up for meals and the other was used for a meeting place.

Peter moved inside the building and fixed himself a comfortable, warm place to sleep. But the renovation was far from being fully realized. The next projects on the slate were to build a septic system and tank, remove the stucco wall and eliminate trash from the inside rooms. Then they needed to add electrical work and install a heating system including heating under the floors.

During the winter months, Peter and his group of helpers were able to run electricity inside the building and dig the septic system. The official status of the building was documented as "abandoned" when purchased, but after many meetings with lawyers, they were able to officially change the status of the building to "livable"!

Peter, Irina, and the team were preparing to host up to 400 people in the summer of 2021, and they wanted to get the patios ready to use as a dining area. The team planned to build decks, level out a parking area, prepare an area for the tents, clear land for a separate camp for the children, and clear out an area for sports.

Inside, the debris needed to be cleared out before the concrete floor could be poured. There was a lot to remove from the removed stucco on the walls, the ceiling, and other leftovers from construction. Two sets of stairs were built to the second floor, replacing the temporary ladders. Surrounding the building, concrete slabs that were about six and a half feet wide (and eight inches underground) needed to be dug up. Only after this was done could the team build the large, covered porch areas. They poured concrete on the entire first floor, built walls to divide rooms, bathrooms and showers, dug their own water well, installed windowsills, plastered walls, etc. The work seemed endless! Just writing about it makes me tired.

The remodeling of the inside of the old school continued throughout the next two years and continues even as I write. The grounds were improved, prepared for sports, and a zip line was put in. Someone donated an elaborate iron fence that was installed, and the kid's camp area was built. An outside kitchen has also been constructed, with a separate building containing seven toilets, showers, and 20 sinks were built. The heating has been installed as well as a donated windmill (which is installed and functioning). A large tent, also donated, was erected upon a concrete slab poured by the team. The company that donated the windows and supplies for roofing also decided to cover about 70% of the cost of the heating! God continued to supply their needs!

Peter, Irina and the team continually think of new projects. Such is the way with visionaries. But they could never have imagined that their Ark would become a place to gather people from all over Ukraine during war.

Just like God sent animals into the Ark to be saved, God sends people to The Ark of Ukraine to find food and clothes, healing and hope.

Watch the You Tube video[1] from 2/2/22 to get a glimpse of the camps and raft trips.

[1] "Noah's Ark Ukraine Missions." YouTube, 27 Jan. 2022, youtu.be/ K-CBBCweVac.

Chapter 5: Ark Expansion

In the same way, let your light shine before others, that they will see your good deeds and glorify your Father in heaven. –Matthew 5:16 NIV

He will turn the hearts of the parents to their children, and the hearts of the children to their parents... –Malachi 4:6 NIV

Men's and Women's Camps

While meeting the needs of children who have had limited (or no) exposure to the gospel, it was impossible for Peter and Irina to not notice the needs of the adults. They prayed yearly for what God's plans were, and they were led, year after year, to begin new ministries. The overwhelming successful children's camps gave them confidence that they could also meet some of the other needs they saw around them. They sought God in prayer, after all God was their partner. It was God's idea in the first place, so they knew He would show them the next steps. A missionary friend used to say, "God's will, God's bill," indicating a trust in God for providing everything you need.

Confident that He hears our prayers, Peter and Irina discerned that women's and men's camps needed be offered. The planning they were accustomed to doing began anew. They met with their teams, prayed, fasted and planned every detail of the camp. They interviewed speakers for the messages and chose the one who was the best fit. They developed various teams, each planning their part of the camp: sports, food/cooking, service, leadership, and music.

Years of interacting with individuals in their homes unveiled a common necessity-to inspire and support people in their faith journey, and to motivate them to actively pursue the divine plan for their lives. They began holding men's and women's camps in the summer of 2009, women's camps in 2012. This was followed by father-son camps and mother-daughter camps. In 2021, they held five different camps.

Within one day of opening registration for camp. they reached their full capacity! The Noah's Ark team members were surprised by how many new people (and how many unbelievers) had heard about the camp and signed up. The camp wasn't advertised except by word of mouth.

For example, one girl heard about the camp from a friend and called to register while she was still at work. All her coworkers heard her on the phone and one after another realized they wanted to attend as well. So, 11 people ended up registering from that office. It is amazing how God works!

During the four to five-day women's camps, the leadership team served faithfully and tirelessly. Their love was expressed through their patience and support of one another and by their unconditional love of the attendees. They heard many women speaking about how God worked in their hearts through their time at camp.

One girl said, "I never knew God and now I'm sure that I know Him. I want to change my lifestyle and my family's lifestyle." Many lives were changed, owing to the time they spent focusing on their relationship with God and with each other.

Mother and Daughter Camp

When the team was planning the mother-daughter camp, they didn't realize how impactful the camp would be. Families arrived in tears and fears, worried about the four days when mothers and daughters would sleep in one tent together, spending so much time together. This was not a typical experience for many of the attending mothers or daughters. Some people are fortunate to have grown up having a close relationship with their mothers. However, for many that is not the case.

During camp, they saw mothers and daughters cry together, laugh together, and have conversations that they'd never been able to have before. Relationships were built, restored, and strengthened. It was such a special time, an amazing thing to witness for the team, and a sacred experience for the participants.

One mother and daughter who attended camp, shared that their relationship had been estranged. They hadn't had much communication for the past two years. The mother thought that her daughter, who was in her teenage years at the time, would eventually just grow out of what she thought was only a stage. During the time at the camp, she listened to the discussions, and searched her own heart. That mother realized the breakdown in their relationship was because of her own attitude. She had been trying to control her daughter too much, trying to make her daughter more like herself rather than accepting her daughter as she was.

They forgave each other and found a renewed respect and love for one another. Communication and relationship restored, they left feeling hopeful and determined to maintain this open communication and respect for each other.

Another mother, who came with her daughter, was grateful for the time she and her daughter spent together without the distractions of everyday responsibilities. After listening to the different topics, she desired to work on her relationships with her own mother and mother-in-law.

During these mother-daughter camps, Irina had time to minister to women individually, if needed. One mother confided to Irina about the adulterous relations she had been having with different men over several years. This woman woke up and realized how the lies and consequences of sin were affecting her daughter and her whole family. Convicted of her sins, she repented to God and in front of Irina, then she deleted and blocked numbers and emails of these men.

Many stories came from these camps, showing how the Lord worked in their lives to restore relationships and strengthen their faith. For every camp attendee, there was at least one miracle story of how God met them at their point of need. How many mothers and daughters could benefit from a camp like this?

Men's Camps

In November of 2021, God gathered men of different backgrounds, denominations, ages, and beliefs at the Ark. The team saw the Lord's hand in every single aspect of the camp. He shined through choosing the topics to discuss, through the worship, the small groups, and the activities. Many men recommitted their lives to the Lord. Some accepted Jesus as Lord and Savior for the first time. What a joy to witness lives being changed!

Two men were baptized on the last day of camp. One of the men had been coming to church with his mother for a few years, but his father's example of a Christian was a stumbling block for him. This man was taking drugs and drinking a lot of alcohol. And he was one of the hardest people to get along with at camp, according to the leaders. The Lord really started working in his life, and the team could see something changing in him. A short time before he attended the men's camp, he gave his life to Jesus during a church service. He expressed a strong desire to be baptized. The man heard about our camps and asked if he could serve at the women's retreat, but the team decided to invite him to the men's retreat instead.

It was at that men's camp that he accepted Jesus as his Lord and Savior. He also desired to be baptized. After being baptized at camp, he started attending church regularly and has become an active member of that church.

One men's camp stands out as being the most unique in Peter's mind. In this camp, many who came had been drug addicts, alcoholics, and men who were currently in rehabilitation. One special soldier, Dima, came and shared his story. He was at war, away from his family, when he learned that his son quit serving in the Ukrainian army and began serving in the Russian army. He was conflicted. Dima couldn't fight against his own son, and he couldn't support Russia. He deserted the army and ended up arriving in

Vinnytsia, where he was taken to a rehab center. At the rehab center, God started working on his heart. He somehow found out about our camp There, he found forgiveness and peace.

Peter also had a dear friend join them at camp. This man had stopped taking communion for 20 years because he felt he wasn't worthy of God. Peter shared with him that people don't come to God already clean, but that everyone comes to God as sinners. He explained that only God can change a person, and He does that from the inside out.

God can give one a new heart if they ask him to.

This man finally understood the love and forgiveness of God. He understood that there was nothing he could do to earn or deserve God's love, but that God gives His love freely. Finally, the man was able to take communion with a heart of gratitude and love.

Another unique factor within this camp was that nine pastors from various churches in Ukraine attended. It was highly unusual to have different denominations fellowshipping and worshipping together. The men laid down their "right to be right" and took up the mandate to love and honor fellow brothers in Christ. Everyone got to experience the truth.

"How good and pleasant it is when brothers live together in unity!" (Psalms 133:1 NIV)

After this camp, they had a follow-up Bible study where over 60 men attended. These men continue to fellowship with one another.

Family Camp

The Lord guided Peter and Irina to hold a family camp June 14, 2021 as a unique way to reach out to their community. The Noah's Ark team invited both believers and non-believers to fellowship with one another during the four-day tent camp. The team had been organizing these camps for almost a decade, and the Lord has continually blessed their efforts and expanded them through the years.

The cost of this camp would normally be prohibitive for most families, but Noah's Ark camps were arranged to cost only a small amount. This camp was designed to disciple believers while evangelizing to those who did not yet know the Lord. And there was a separate camp for the children running concurrently. This allowed parents to be able to hear from God without distractions. It was also a great opportunity to teach children the gospel. Out of the 400 attendees, around 170 were children with ages spanning from 3 to 16 years. They were divided into distinct groups with a dedicated team managing the children's camp. That team of adults (and trained teenagers) accompanied the youth from morning until bedtime.

These gatherings were not affiliated with any specific church or denomination; instead, they welcomed all individuals interested in participating. Attendees came from various faith backgrounds, including Baptist, Pentecostal, charismatic, Catholic, orthodox, and others. Witnessing Christians from diverse traditions gradually developed love and unity despite their theological differences was truly inspiring. They discovered they all shared a common bond—their deep love for Jesus. The community transformed into a group of disciples actively involved in making more disciples. Numerous home groups sprouted because of these gatherings, which served as a powerful testimony to non-believers who witnessed the unity of faith.

The genuine display of God's love was evident through authentic, everyday relationships. Numerous individuals learned about God, and many Christians rededicated their lives to the Lord during this blessed camping event. The experience evoked tears of both conviction and joy, with everyone attributing all glory to God.

Despite the physical challenges and the exhaustion of what turned out to be their largest camp ever, the Lord moved powerfully. Participants and leaders persevered through seemingly impossible moments. God provided the strength needed, and amidst the difficulties, they felt a profound sense of joy, expressing gratitude and praise for all that God accomplished.

The first day of camp, just as everyone was arriving, it started raining and hailing. The Noah's Ark team thought that with that kind of weather, everyone would just load right back up and head home. To their surprise, everyone stuck it out! Everyone waited for the rain to pass before setting up tents.

A former atheist attended the men's camp, having learned about the camp during a conversation with Peter while he was repairing Peter's car. The man decided to come and brought four other non-believers with him. The first couple of days, he was very timid about listening and joining the teaching time; he sat far away so no one could see him. But slowly, he started getting more connected. He fully joined the last two sessions.

After camp, he called Peter crying, sharing that he was so touched by the way everyone served and loved so selflessly. He said he never believed that God existed until coming to camp and that it would be impossible to love and serve without having a relationship with God.

Another man who attended camp had studied at a seminary, serving in ministry most of his life. The topic of camp was about connecting with God on a deeper level. The team taught about not just going through the motions of attending church and learning information about God and the Bible. Because of camp, this man felt convicted by his lack of hunger for God. On the last day of camp, he shared with everyone that he wanted to rededicate his life to the Lord. He wanted to leave his empty, lukewarm relationship with God.

I could relate to this story very well, as I had a similar experience.

Upon conversion, I joined Arcade Baptist Church and learned so much about God. I attended 2-3 Bible studies a week and I learned many things. I even learned how to ask the question, "Do you have a personal relationship with Jesus Christ?" to non-believers. I knew that, if they answered in the negative, I would then offer them the plan of salvation. But I wasn't so sure that I did things right because I was just going through the motions. I wanted to be honest with God, so I never sang the words, "I love you, Lord." I didn't want to lie, and I didn't know if I truly loved God. When I was at a prayer retreat, I witnessed a room full of women worshipping and loving God with all their hearts!

I wanted that!

I became hungry for what they had. God heard me and answered the cry of my heart. Blessed are they that hunger for they will be filled.[1] Sometime later, I had the experience of feeling the love of God; I was engulfed in His presence and filled with the Holy spirit! This was life-changing for me! I now know that I love God and that He loves me. And I love to share with others. There is always more of God if you want it.

Are you hungry for more?

[1] Matthew 5:6

Endless Ministry Opportunities

Peter and Irina have an amazing amount of energy and inspiration as they think of how to share the love of the Lord every day in every way. They are always thinking about ways to bless their community and show their love by their actions.

In 2020, during the regulated COVID 19 shutdown, Peter built a blessing box in front their home in Vinnytsia. It was a three-shelf box, like a cupboard on legs. One shelf was for books, another was for food and the third was for toys. Also, one year, when Peter got a mountain bike for his birthday, he started taking groups mountain biking., He used the time for witnessing about the love of God and answering questions the men had. Peter is always ready to share the gospel as quickly as he shares his home, his food and his time.

After Noah's Ark acquired the schoolhouse, they began gathering friends and local villagers to share stories and thank God for all that He had done (and was currently doing). They took time to remember God's miracles through every day, every camp, and every project. God made the impossible possible. They gave thanks that they could be a part of the work that God was doing in Ukraine.

Noah's Ark ministered to the people in the nearby village giving them gifts of chickens at Christmas, inviting them to events held at the Ark and offering friendship and help when needed.

In February and March of 2014, Russia invaded and subsequently annexed the Crimean Peninsula[1] from Ukraine (the Ukrainian military, as of this writing, continues fighting Russian expansion over eastern territories). Concerned about the people there, Peter, Irina and the team visited the war zone, and they helped both soldiers and citizens when they visited.

At Christmas, they took presents into the demilitarized zone. Peter and his team gave gifts to children of Ukrainian soldiers as well as to children of Russian soldiers. They repaired houses damaged in the fighting so the families could resume some form of normalcy and live in a space that could be warm and dry. They gifted soldiers serving on the front lines with warm coats, new socks, food, friendship and hope. Many soldiers were strengthened during their visits.

One year, the Noah's Ark team met one pastor who rode a bicycle to help people in need. After a year, Peter was able to purchase a car for him through donations from many supporters. Now with a car, that pastor was able to help many more people, which he was anxious to do. Non-believers come to get food, and many also attended church services to hear about Jesus. Peter and Irina have helped to develop 11 house churches! As the war escalated, they also started ministering in the hospital. Because of the war, people began to think about life and death and subsequently come to a saving knowledge of Jesus Christ. We rejoice that their lives are hidden in Christ.

"Every single year we worried," Irina reflects. "We didn't know how we were going to be able accomplish our plans and projects. However, as it turns out, we really didn't have to worry at all, because God is faithful to us. He has always covered our needs! We didn't have a clear understanding of how we would be able to accomplish our visions, but God has always provided. It's a huge miracle what God has done this last year; God provided for so many people affected by the war. We didn't know if we were going to see the next day or not. We didn't have a budget set. We couldn't plan not knowing if we would live to see the next day. But God had a plan, and He provided the means to buy food and supplies for the people in need. There were so many people praying for us, for the people in Ukraine, and helping us."

[1] "Crimean Peninsula." *Encyclopædia Britannica*, Encyclopædia Britannica, inc., 14 Feb. 2024, www.britannica.com/place/Crimean-Peninsula.

Chapter 6: Partners and Builders

The godly people in the land are my true heroes! I take pleasure in them! –Psalms 16:3 NLT

I planted the seed in your hearts, and Apollos watered it, but it was God who made it grow. It's not important who does the planting, or who does the watering. What's important is that God makes the seed grow. The one who plants and the one who waters work together with the same purpose. And both will be rewarded for their own hard work. For we are both God's workers. And you are God's field. You are God's building. –1 Corinthians 3:6-9 NLT

Many Hands Needed

If you take the time to observe the credits rolling at the conclusion of a movie, you might find yourself amazed by the sheer number of individuals who played a part in bringing the final production to life. This same sentiment holds true for the Noah's Ark Mission, Ukraine.

Numerous individuals have been (and continue to be) instrumental in its success and resilience. Those people came alongside Peter and Irina had their eyes opened to the needs of people in Ukraine and the ways God could meet those needs. The people mentioned here are but a few of the many who obeyed the promptings of the Holy Spirit. Some had a passion to share the gospel to every corner of the world; some were willing to invest their money and time. Everyone seemed to have invested their prayers toward the success of the vision of the Noah's Ark Mission, Ukraine. Without many workers and partners in prayer, faith, finances, and labor, this mission would not have been possible, nor would it have impacted even a tenth of the lives it has so clearly touched. All those who partnered with the mission will share in its reward. They are all building for the same God and for His purposes.

Alfred (Al) and Georgine Yeatts

Among these remarkable individuals, Al and Georgine Yeatts stand out as contributors to the mission's achievements. Both the Tkachuks and the Yeatts family were forever changed because of their friendship with each other.

Alfred Yeatts was born on October 31, 1934, in Texas on a ranch. He moved with his parents to Southern California during the depression, living in various Southern California areas until they settled in Ontario. That's where Al met Georgine. It was during their sophomore year of JP High School in Ontario, California. Al was raised in a Christian family and their dating amounted to attending Youth for Christ events every Saturday night, often accompanied by his parents.

Georgine Cherbak Yeatts was born in Upland, California on September 9, 1934. Her paternal family came from Russia in 1899 and became ranchers and farmers in various parts of California. They raised different crops also. First, they started raising potatoes, but that didn't last long. They had orchards of apricots, peaches, lemons and oranges, grapefruit, different kinds of grapes, almonds, and olives on their land when they finally settled.

Georgine's mother was a Christian who went to church, but her father did not. When Georgine went to church camp at the age of 14, her grandfather happened to be at the camp as well. He introduced her to the Lord and to the life of faith. He was so worried about Georgine's mom because she was married to a non-Christian; that was always a sore spot in their relationship.

Al and Georgine got married in 1955, when they were sophomores in college. After they were married, on June 10th, they moved to Redlands where Al worked for a Grand Central rocket company. Eventually, Al became an engineer for Aerojet in Sacramento. They gave birth to three children and fostered several more. Al joined the

Gideons, and that group became a big part of their lives. As a couple, the Yeatts were always interested in outreach and missions, which made for a divine meeting with Paul and Irina. They were introduced to the Tkachuks during a mission's conference at Arcade Church in Sacramento, California, where they were attending.

While Al and Georgine were manning a Gideon booth at the conference, they had the opportunity to meet Max Kusch, who approached them to express his gratitude for the Gideon Bible ministry. This encounter peaked Georgine's curiosity, prompting her to look further into their new friend.

Max, a Ukrainian national, shared his personal story of receiving a New Testament Gideon Bible from someone crossing the Russian border. It was during the time when he was stationed as a guard there. The giver not only handed him the life-transforming book, but also explained the gospel of Jesus Christ to him and how to enter the Kingdom of God. Intrigued by the man's claims, Max examined the book. Heading the call of his heart, Max surrendered his life to Jesus Christ. After that time Max harbored a strong desire to share this Good News to the people in his hometown in Ukraine.

During their conversation, Max mentioned Peter and Irina. Shortly thereafter, Al and Georgine had the opportunity to meet and assist Peter and Irina as they adjusted to a new country and culture. The Yeatts provided the Tkachuks with English lessons and guidance. The two families spent considerable time together sharing lessons, activities, meals, prayers and dreams.

Over time, Al and Georgine formed a deep bond with Peter and Irina, considering them to be the closest friends they had ever had. Georgine was profoundly impressed by Peter's unwavering dedication to God. According to her, he had a visionary mindset on how to reach people with the Good News of Jesus Christ. Peter possessed a remarkable ability to disregard discouraging messages that suggested certain tasks were impossible. In this regard, Al and Peter shared a similar outlook. Meanwhile, Irina, akin to Georgine (although being somewhat skeptical), embraced their plans with a positive attitude and without any complaints.

Al and Georgine embarked on 13 trips to Ukraine with the Tkachuks. It was not only their deep connection to Peter and Irina that prompted Al and Georgine to go to Ukraine, but also their sense of adventure. When Peter and Irina started a rafting and camping ministry adventure, Al and Georgine were ready, willing, and able! They leaped at the adventure of it all. They both felt the rafting trips were a wonderful opportunity for them to minister for the Lord together.

"You never know when Alfred's Boy Scout skills might come in handy!" quipped Georgine.

The Yeatts were impressed by the way that the Tkachuks were continually ministering. There was seemingly no offseason for them. Al and Georgine were impressed with the fact that Peter and Irina started teaching the Bible to neighboring teenagers shortly after they were married. Their mutual love and respect for one another knit their hearts together.

Max and Lilia Kusch and Ministering in Polohy

Max became a Christian in 1995 while serving in the Soviet Army. A fellow soldier had given him a Gideon's New Testament as a gift while standing guard at the wall. Max married Lilia in 1996 and immigrated to Sacramento in 1997.

In June 2005, Al and Georgine decided to travel to Ukraine with Max and his wife. The 2005 trip to Polohy[1] was an answer to the desire that Max Kusch had about sharing the gospel of Jesus Christ. He wished to share the Good News (that had changed his life) with the people in the town where he was raised. He planned to join the Noah's Ark team and conduct two children's camps in the area.

Just knowing that God wants you to do a work doesn't mean that it will be easy. Reaching the lost is not without opposition and struggles. Some trips take unexpected twists and opposition will come. Sometimes there is testing. A missionary must take out time from their normal, perhaps comfortable lives, travel for days, wait, wait some more, and navigate strange confusing travel arrangements. The situation becomes a battle of faith over fear. Missionaries may sleep in various strange places, try to communicate with those who speak a different language, eat strange food, and at times, face danger. There may even be a temptation to believe that God didn't really prompt them to go.

Max Kushch faced all of this and more.

Max and his wife Lilia, along with Al and Georgine Yeatts, flew into Budapest, Hungary from the US to purchase a van for ministry. They met Lilia's uncle at the airport. It had taken him two days to get through the border from Ukraine. At that time, it was not uncommon to wait three days in line to cross the border. The Kushches arrived on a later flight because Lilia had gotten lost in the airport and missed her original flight. Al and Georgine had problems going through customs. It was their faith (and prayer) which got them all through. Al and Georgine left the US on June 14th, but it was June 16th before they reached the border.

Lilla's uncle took them to his home, then Max and his uncle went to take care of the paperwork for the vehicle. After that, the two men went to the garage to get the van outfitted and legally ready to go. There were many plans, hopes, and dreams to be fulfilled with that van. It was an answer to much prayer. After a week's delay, they were all on their way to Vinnytsia. They were going to drive the van into Ukraine to be used for ministry.

The plan was to pick up a car that had been purchased for the Noah's Ark Missions and drive it to the base in Vinnytsia, then minister at the camp in Polohy. The team would be in the Zaporizhzhia region toward eastern Ukraine[2]. The route they were taking would lead them through Odessa. Georgine's father's family from Russia had had a summer home there. Georgine was very excited and anticipated seeing this beautiful area.

After Max took them to the border wall where he was saved, they traveled through the Carpathian Mountains. While driving at night through the town of Ternopble, they discovered it was the first day of a two-day holiday and many people were in their cups[3]. One young man and his wife were arguing, and he stepped into the street just as they drove by. The new van hit the drunk man, and he died on the side of the road. In shock, everyone waited for the police to arrive. When they did, the police took their statements. They were very courteous but also intimidating, and threatened Max not to contact the American embassy. Max collapsed in shock and was taken to the hospital.

It was a dark night.

What was going to happen to them? It was so hard not to think the worst. If Max had to go to jail, how long would he have to be there? How could their plans proceed? And what of his family? God had a plan already in motion. The next morning, they all were astonished, relieved and overjoyed at the sight of some of the men from Peter's church. They had driven all night from Vinnytsia, after hearing of their plight. After these men paid a bribe to the police, Max was able to leave.

Many who read this will have a reaction of some kind. Some will say that a bribe should never be paid ever for any reason (as it is not honest, not the right thing to do). Then, there are those who will understand that when a person is dealing with a dishonest government official whose wages are meager, a bribe might just be the only thing keeping a person out of jail. Perhaps that bribe will keep someone from having to pay even more to get out. It is not an easy decision to make. Working in other countries requires making very difficult decisions. For the van mission to continue, Max had to be released. Regardless of what your opinion is I do hope you have a measure of understanding and grace for the decision that was made.

Wanting to give his condolences and to express his regret, Max approached the family of the man who had died. Forgiveness wasn't on these people's minds, and some of the men chased Max with a pitchfork ready to do great damage! Max managed to escape and resume his travel plans to bring the gospel to the children of Polohy.

Because of the great opposition, everyone knew that the mission to serve in the Polohy area was going to be an important part of God's plan. The van was released but needed repairs before being used or sold—but God.

Things may seem hopeless—but God.

Terrors and horrors abound—but God.

Our strength fails—but God.

All is hopeless, but God has surely listened and heard our cry. Praise be to God who has not rejected our prayer or withheld his love from us!

[1] Polohy is a city in Zaporizhzia Oblast, Ukraine. The population of Polohy at that time was about 18,000 people. It was known for its sunflower oil extraction and its fertile plains.

[2] "Zaporizhzhya." *Encyclopædia Britannica*, Encyclopædia

Britannica, inc., 15 Apr. 2024, www.britannica.com/place/Zaporizhzhya-Ukraine.

[3] To be "in their cups" means to be drunk.

Alex Mayacky

Max met a seminary graduate, Alex Mayacky, who agreed to become a church pastor in Polohy. Max and Lilia supported his ministry from that time until (as of this writing). In 2003, Alexis's team organized a children's Christian day camp in the summer and a Christmas Experience theatrical play in the wintertime. Pastor Alex facilitated Christian outreach, educational programs, and Sunday services at the pastor's apartment or at rented facilities. In 2004, church membership was growing but without a church facility, it presented a huge challenge. Pastor Alex and a few dedicated helpers conducted outreach in colleges and schools, also. But because proclamation of the Christian message was forbidden in public places, they instead presented educational programs which discussed harmful effects of abortion, smoking, drinking, and other health related topics. After these presentations, Pastor Alex invited interested individuals to attend church events or to come to his house for Bible study. At that time, Alex hoped to find a permanent church building and to run a Christian based orphanage.

Alex's mother was a Christian, but his father had fallen away from the faith and had fallen into alcoholism. In his youth, Alex ran with the crowd that drank and took illegal drugs. At around the age of 14, Alex had a dream where he was shown the horrors of hell. He woke up, afraid and shaken. A short time later, he had another meaningful dream. In this dream, he saw Christ crucified. These dreams changed the trajectory of Alex's life. It was after that that he gave his life to Christ.

As an adult, Alex pursued a career as a professional soccer player, but by 2005, Alex had had three heart attacks which occurred after he was body building and lifting weights. He was disheartened as his body eventually succumbed to wear and tear, but God's call to reach the lost satisfied his heart. Alex attended seminary with the same dedication that he played sports.

Answering the call to be a pastor in Polohy, Alex was concerned with the destruction by drugs and alcohol that he saw in people's lives. It was so prevalent in the town of Polohy. The city housed many unwed mothers and broken families as well. His heart was to make a difference in these people's lives the way Christ had made a difference in his. He also was no stranger to miracles.

Alex's wife accidentally smashed her fingers so badly that the doctor wanted to remove some of them, but they had no money for surgery. Alex and his wife then went to the university and a doctor there agreed to do the surgery for considerably less. Alex and his wife prayed fervently that evening. The next day after his class, Alex went to get his wife and take her for surgery, but her hand had healed completely! There was not even a bruise left! God is a miracle-working God!

Fast forward to March of 2023, when Polohy was captured by Russian forces. Alex and his family were able to escape and Max supports Alex's new church in a different location now. Max's father was not able to get out and sadly, several of Max's relatives were killed. Several of the men and women who had attended the camp in 2005 died as well.

"The school where we conducted the camps has been flattened," informed Max, "and much of this city has been destroyed. Thankfully, the face of the city changed before capture. A church had been established, people had repented and given up their drinking and drugs, an orphanage had been established. People started going to church, getting free of their sinful ways, and started a completely new life because of the small camps. The people in the town were all talking about it. Because word of the work that was being done spread rapidly, Alex was given a spot on a radio talk show. He had permission by the government to talk and to share the Good News of Jesus Christ. There were close to 600,000 listeners to that show. 'Like a small rock pushing against a bigger rock.' It is doubtful that we will ever know the ways in which lives were impacted by the children's camps," Max told us. "I'm so thankful that God did a mighty work in this city before it was invaded. I believe hope was planted in that soil and will continue to grow despite the grim situation."

Some plant, and some water, but God provides the increase.

When a person accepts the blood sacrifice of Jesus Christ and becomes a Christian, he or she is given gifts to be used for building up and encouragement of the body of Christ—other believers. Some, like Andrew Romanov, have been given the ability to create wealth and the gift of giving. He also is a teacher and a pastor.

Alex has been given the gift of teaching and pastoring. Max has a passion for evangelism. Al and Georgine have gifts of hospitality, evangelism, wisdom and mercy. Some of the gifts mentioned in the Bible are teaching, exhortation, leadership, mercy, healing, helps, evangelism, preaching, hospitality, prophesy, wisdom, faith, tongues, interpretation of tongues, miracles, discernment, etc. These gifts can be seen as they are expressed in the lives of believers.

Other people with many gifts have contributed in various ways to build up and encourage the ministry of Noah's Ark Missions, Ukraine.

Arcade Church

Arcade Church, in Sacramento California, has been a generous and consistent supporter of Noah's Ark since its inception. When Irina and Peter first came to the US, they joined Arcade Church. Their friends, Max and Lillia, attended, and this is where they met Al and Georgine Yeatts, Dan and Darlene Bryant, Andrew and Sarah Romonov, Carl Till, and many other supporters.

The Noah's Ark board members in the US are instrumental to the mission's success. They help carry out the organizational and business aspects of this non-profit organization. The Noah's Ark's current board members that attend Arcade (at present) are Joel and Liz Kaspick, and Mary Ann and Jim Olson. The board is so blessed to have these faithful servants. Not only do they serve well, but they are also generous givers of their resources and their talents. Another board member did not want to be mentioned here, but she is a great asset to the ministry as well. Everyone brings their own gifts and abilities to the table.

Mary Ann and Jim Olson

Mary Ann explains how they got involved with the mission:

"We were introduced to Peter and Irina Tkachuk and Noah's Ark Ministry by our friends, Al and Georgine Yeatts. [It was] in 2018 at a share and prayer meeting at their home. Peter and Irina shared their summer outreach ministry with young people with river rafting and camping trips. We were drawn to their testimonies of God's love and guidance and protection and blessing to those who attended the camps. In 2019, Jim started helping Georgine and Al with accounting and email communications to those who were supporting the ministry with funds and prayers. We see God at work in every part of this faith ministry. We are blessed to get to be part of it."

Jim is the man behind the money and keeps accounts of the donations, expenses, and taxes. Fortunately, he now has Joel to collaborate with.

Joel and Liz Kaspick

Joel and Liz stepped in to fill the void Peter and Irina felt when Al Yeatts passed, becoming generous supporters of the mission. They are passionate about sharing their excitement over what Peter and Irina are doing in Ukraine with others.

"My husband Joel and I were first introduced to Peter and Irina Tkachuk as part of a small group in the home of good friends Carolyn and Bob Clark," tells Liz. "The Tkachuks had moved to Sacramento several years before and made Arcade their church home. By the time we met them, they were taking people back to Ukraine with them each summer to facilitate vacation Bible Schools for children.

"This work had not been on my radar. However, by the time we left the Clark's home that evening, I knew that we needed to support Peter and Irina in their ministry. Their story of dedicating their lives completely to the Lord was one we could not ignore. They were such a witness of what it means to pray, wait on the Lord, and trust His leading.

"This past week, I read Isaiah 55:1-3. Listen to what God says to the people through Isaiah.

Come, all you who are thirsty, come to the waters; and you who have no money, come, buy and eat! Come buy wine and milk without money and without cost. Why spend money on what is not bread, and your labor on what does not satisfy? Listen, listen to me, and eat what is good, and you will delight in the richest of fare. Give ear and come to me: listen, that you may live. (NIV)

"Jesus is the Living Water. Jesus is the Bread of Life. Those who seek Him will never hunger or thirst. Peter and Irina Tkachuk have believed and accepted that invitation and are living all in and all out every day to share it with others.

"In Sacramento, we help by collecting goods–food, clothing,

bedding, flashlights, hygienic supplies, etc. to send in shipping containers to the camp. What is collected also needs to be sorted and packed. Recently, we were involved in holding a fund-raising event so the outbuildings at the camp could be completed. This was just one more opportunity to watch God at work through His Church—the body of Christ—using people's God-given talents to work together. We are grateful for faithful people who will continue to support what God is doing through the Tkachuks in Ukraine. The road ahead will be a difficult one, and in the words of the song, we do not know what the future holds, but we know Who holds the future. And in following Him, we 'will delight in the richest fare.'"[1]

[1] Isaiah 55:1

The Vlasovas

Vera Vlasova and her husband Andry Vlasov are very helpful to Peter and Irina, especially when they are in Sacramento and when loading the shipping containers. Vera is a great companion to Irina and has become like a sister to her.

Vera and her husband came to the US from Russia in 1995 with their one-year-old daughter, looking for a better life. Vera met Irina in the spring of 2013 and that summer, Vera found herself in Ukraine helping with the camps. She has gone back each year for ten years since then to help. Vera loves being at the Ark where she always receives a warm welcome. She describes it as a home away from home with family.

The widow's and mothers of fallen soldier's camp the summer of 2023 touched her. "When the women came," Vera reflects, "they were depressed and looked down, but after three days they were laughing and running, their heads held high!" Vera's faith grows stronger and stronger each year as she participates in the camps and realizes what God can do. She encourages everyone to tell others about the love and the healing that God can bring.

"Share the gospel of Jesus Christ!" says Vera. "It is the most important thing!"

Carl Till

In the beginning, when Peter and Irina began to dream together with Al and Georgine about what ministry they could do in Ukraine, Carl Till set up an organization, Euro Christian Partners[1], so they could begin receiving donations to begin ministry. The members of Arcade Church in Sacramento, although not the only supporter of Noah's Ark Mission, have been a huge benefactor from the beginning. Many members provided monthly finances, as well as finances for special projects (including the funds needed to purchase the school building in 2019). Members and other donors donated goods to fill the shipping containers. They gave of their time, their prayer, and their love and friendship. The new mission's pastor, Tom Norris, and many of the Arcade Church members continue to promote and generously support the Noah's Ark Mission.

[1] https://eurochristianpartners.org/

Dan Bryant

The missions pastor, Dan Bryant, at Arcade Church during the mission's formation, likens Irina and Peter to modern day George Mullers[1]. They prayed and God provided.

Dan exclaimed, "There is a story in Mueller's biography about how they needed heat in an orphanage and miraculously God provided someone to install heat for the children. Likewise, someone donated and finished putting in the radiant floor heating in the Tkachuk's camp building! What a timely and providential work of God!"

[1] "The Life of George Muller." GeorgeMuller.Org, www.georgemuller.org/devotional/the-life-of-george-muller. Accessed 7 May 2024.

Andrew and Sarah Romanov

The Romanovs were one of the couples who partnered with the Tkachuks from the beginning. Andrew was born in Russia in 1973, moved to Ukraine when he was nine, then immigrated with his family to the United States in 1983. Andrew and Sarah met Peter and Irina through Max Kusch at Arcade Church. The couple were attending when Peter and Irina came in 2005.

Sarah explains, "From the beginning of our marriage, Andrew and I have recognized the value of giving to the Lord's work around the world. We have supported various missionaries and ministries over the years as God provided and enabled us to give. Once we met and got to know Peter and Irina, we saw their love for the people of Ukraine and their commitment to serve. We were glad to support Noah's Ark and the work they do. In 2018, we got a chance to travel to Ukraine to help the Noah's Ark team with a children's camp in a village, and this personal involvement cemented our commitment to support the ministry. We view ourselves as conduits, through which God can pour His resources. And we ask Him for wisdom in who to support. Giving to the ministry of Noah's Ark, and praying for Peter and Irina and their team, is something we have been very glad to do, and plan to continue doing!"

The two couples, the Tkachuks and Romanovs, connected through the Slavic ministry of Arcade Church. In the context of the small group that Andrew was leading in his home, they became friends. The two couples had the same heart and passion for ministry. Andrew and Sarah saw the single-mindedness of the Tkachuks' hearts and their hard-working sacrifice to serve the purposes of God's Kingdom. They wanted to be a part of that dynamic to serve people. Andrew was able to serve during a men's camp in Ukraine in September of 2021 and was a blessing to the men there. While he was there, he introduced Peter to a company that he knows in Ukraine. The owner of this company came out to the school building, saw the work they were doing, and decided to donate the windows and supplies for roofing, completely free!

Another unexpected blessing!

Andrew was instrumental in providing the logistics to send shipping containers to Ukraine through his company D.C. Transport. Peter and Irina desperately needed a car to continue their ministry. That prayer was answered quickly when a car was donated!

What started as a desire to ship this car to Ukraine, turned into the shipment of six shipping containers of goods to Ukraine. The items were to be used in the ministry of Noah's Ark and the building of the camp over the next few years. The first container was shipped in 2021, before the larger invasion of Russia in February of 2022. They didn't want to just ship a car and leave empty space, so they asked for donations. Peter and Irina made a list of things that would be helpful. Some of these things were donated and others were purchased. When they finally started packing the container, they realized that they did not have room for the car! They ended up just sending the vehicle separately through another company that specifically shipped vehicles.

After the war started with Russia, the second container was shipped, filled with goods and essential supplies for the people of Ukraine. People were so willing to help, and donations flooded in. Since that time, several more containers have been shipped to Ukraine, all filled with humanitarian aid and items to be used for the building and ministry. No one had any idea of how much these supplies would be needed.

Irina has seen the larger view of the container ministry. She was asked if it wouldn't be easier just to ask for monetary donations and buy the goods. Irina thought about how that statement was true. It would be easier not to spend days in the US, sorting and packing goods for the container. It would be easier to not have to deal with the unpacking, organizing and shipping of the goods in Ukraine. But she sees what a ministry it really is for those in the US and those in Ukraine.

In the US, people have an opportunity to donate both large and small amounts of goods. They can come together to sort, pack and load the container. I, Lura, have found this to be true. "I have enjoyed that activity myself; it is fun to be a part of something so grand! Also, I was able to gather special presents to be given out to widows during camps. My friends and I felt closer to those women and their grief. I like to imagine the joy I can bring with just a simple gift. Like it says in scripture, 'If one member suffers, all suffer together, if one member is honored, all rejoice together.'"[1]

Irina considered the container ministry in Ukraine, as it too blessed those involved. People come to help every weekend and stay. She calls it a mini retreat. They help with the sorting and packaging of goods, which include prayer. After a day of hard work, they take a meal together and talk, sharing their hearts. The mix of believers and non-believers is providential. Many who come to help leave with hope.

Andrew and Peter decided that it would be cheaper to buy the containers instead of renting them, due to the cost of shipping back an empty container. The cost of a container has varied over the years from $7,500 to 4,000. Before the war, one company could ship a container all the way to Vinnytsia for about $5500. In 2023, they can't ship directly to the port of Odessa, so it gets shipped to Poland, and is then taken to Vinnytsia. From D.C. Transport in California to Poland in 2023, it cost between $5,000 to $6,000. This is paid for by donations to the Noah's Ark Missions. From Poland to Vinnytsia donations to Connect International pays the approximate $5,000 cost. When not being shipped, the containers are used for other purposes at the camp site.

[1] 1 Corinthians 12:26

Connect International

Connect International[1] is a not-for-profit organization that supports many projects in Ukraine, including a widows and orphans ministry. They also facilitate relief projects, build churches, give emergency aid, etc. Their goal seems to be to restore hope and share the gospel. Information about their many projects and partners can be found on their website of the same name. This is such a good example of ministries working together for the same purpose.

The potential of the containers was not lost on Peter the builder, either.

"Since we now have our own property, we are able to make long-term investments that we know will last. We plan to host camps, conferences, retreats and whatever the Lord has in store for us. We have a desire to do our camps with excellence and strive to grow and bring in new elements. We want to develop our sports and extra activities. This year we are praying for provision to buy two pools, 10 tents, a trampoline, craft supplies, soccer balls and nets, footballs, and volleyballs and nets.

"We will also be able to use the shipping container as an extra storage unit on the property," said Peter. "We plan to build a roof over the top. It will be like a big carport where we can store our tools, landscaping equipment, camp materials, sports equipment, etc. These are very practical improvements that will allow us to minister to hundreds, perhaps thousands of people in the years to come. In our experience, we have seen God work mightily through camps and time spent together there. God has given us the opportunity to work with people and share the hope and love we have because of Christ." It is curious to see how such an unlikely and impractical idea can yield so much fruit!

In 2021, Peter continued to rejoice over God's sovereignty in this letter,

We received the second container and saw yet another miracle from God. Clearing things through customs in Ukraine is always a big hassle and the system is very corrupt. We prayed and asked the Lord to help us and guide us. In one day, we were able to get the container cleared and they didn't even open the container once! We cried tears of joy and thankfulness. Our God is so good and powerful! We are so thankful for every item that was donated. The Lord knew the needs, and we already have been able to share and use many of the items. We are so thankful for the opportunity to serve in Ukraine and that God has entrusted us with this mission. We are also thankful for you and all that you are doing to help build the Kingdom!

The surprises of generosity continued. They received a little red tractor, which allowed them to do a lot of projects around the camp that previously would have been impossible. A heavy-duty frame tent measuring 80' by 40' was donated and erected before the camps of 2023. And the containers being shipped were such a blessing to them. Many of the items they prayed for were received from the shipping containers and put to good use in the camps.

"Because of your generosity," declared Peter and Irina, "we have been able to continue to provide thousands of people with food and other necessities. Not only are we able to send out packages by mail, but we've also been able to load around five trucks a week that deliver aid to the frontlines."

[1] https://www.connect-inter.com/language/en/

Anna Tyulyu

The Noah's Ark Missions has numerous supporters and volunteers in Ukraine. One of those people is Anna Tyulyu. Anna was born in the eastern part of Ukraine, a place where a train was bombed during the war with Russia. Anna tells the remarkable story of how she came to volunteer at the women's camp during the summer of 2023. God does have mysterious ways in connecting people for his purposes. Anna was the answer to the prayers for this camp for compassionate, skilled counselors who would know how to deal with women experiencing deep grief and sorrow over lost loved ones. Anna's family moved from Ukraine to the US about 25 years prior, but when the war broke out in 2022, Anna's sister, Alina traveled to the Polish border to volunteer her time and to help in whatever way she could. She traveled with a group from the church, House of Bread, in the Sacramento area. She and her group were one of the first ones to set up camps and centers where refugees could gather. They spent three weeks in Poland with this work. Alina then traveled to her hometown in Ukraine and through a friend, connected with the Tkachuks who were sending a lot of humanitarian aid, food, clothes, etc. to their hometown. Back in the US, Alina and Anna were invited to a dinner party where the Tkachuks were attending. This divine set up led Anna to volunteer to help with the women's camp. It's so amazing how God connects people!

Anna and Alina have a legacy of faith.

Their father was a music director in Ukraine and involved with youth and various ways of serving. So was their uncle, who became a pastor in Ukraine. Anna Tyula and Alina have always been involved in ministry from a young age. Their uncle and his wife held summer camps for the youth and Anna would help during her visits with them. Anna went on missionary trips to the northern parts of Russia then married, had a child, and stayed home for a while. Employed as a school social worker in the states, she was always looking out for the needy and those who were struggling. Because her job gave her two months off work during the summer, she tried to go somewhere and volunteer. Her training as a clinician and therapist motivated her to want to help her countrymen in Ukraine.

Anna traveled with her nine-year-old daughter, Aliyah, to volunteer at the camps. This was Aliyah's second trip to Ukraine. Aliyah, a charming and beautiful girl, informed me that she spoke both Russian and Ukrainian. She said the trip was a bit scary in that when there were planes going over them, they were afraid the planes were from Russia. But they weren't. She enjoyed a lot of games, played in the lake, and appreciated the meals. She and her new friends picked some apples and made apple pies. She told of one time, when they were outside, an unexpected cloudburst broke over them and everyone got soaked. They had to scramble for cover of the tents!

When asked if she felt she had changed because of the trip, she replied, "I feel like it kind of changed my heart. When they were teaching us about God, it kind of helped me understand God better." Aliyah said that she ended up with more friends in Ukraine than in the US.

As Aliyah attended the children's program, Anna ministered to the widows and women who had lost a son during combat. Previously, Anna traveled to Poland and spent a month working with refugees. She was hesitant about entering Ukraine during war time, however.

Anna explained, "I was very worried, and I kept praying asking Jesus to protect us and give me peace." When she received peace, she felt completely safe. Driving from Poland, even before they crossed the Ukrainian border, she felt completely at peace. "I just know God takes care of his widows and orphans, and I knew that this kind of work would be something God honors, and that he would protect us. The entire time we were in Ukraine, I was very safe, at least it felt like it was. I didn't feel like I was in a war. There were no bombings around us and very few sirens went off."

Anna is no stranger to loss. She went through a divorce four years prior and grapples with her own losses and pain. She could relate to being a single mother, she could relate to women not having their protector, their person that they rely on around. She wanted to point these widows to God and to Jesus. Listening to the Bible while driving to work one day the verse from Isaiah 54:5 played, the word "husband" caught her ear. She heard that her creator was her husband! She realized that she no longer had to live in fear or shame. God took her out of her grief. She knew then that God would take care of her and that she could talk to him about anything. Jesus was available as her husband to answer questions and provide strength, give wise counsel, and provide for her needs. God would take care of her as his bride. This was a message that she wanted to share with the widows at the camp.

When asked about how it was working with the Tkachuks, Anna replied, "They are people who work so hard and so much. They give 180% to others. They give of themselves, they give what they have, and it's beautiful to see. I know it's a lot of work for them. It's exhausting, but it was encouraging and inspiring to me. They are a good example for others as to how to do ministry. For me it was inspirational; I saw how much effort they put into everything that they put their finger on. They are totally committed to what they do, and they seem to maintain a good attitude while they are doing it. They can keep good relationships with the people they minister to as well."

Anna can be an inspiration for us as well, giving of time and talents, thinking of others more than herself. Anna also is a hero of faith.

Samantha DeGuzman

Two of the many people in Ukraine who have been instrumental to the Noah's Ark Ministries are Samantha DeGuzman and her twin sister, Hope. They partner with Noah's Ark ministries during their camps. Samantha started to help Irina by writing Facebook posts and doing other small tasks for her. Now she helps Irina with administrative tasks, financial reports, and with communication with the states.

Born in the US to a father who was a youth pastor who traveled to do mission trips all around the world, Samantha and her sister were fascinated with Ukraine (out of all the countries that they had visited with their father). The first time the traveled to Ukraine, they were eight years old, over 20 years ago. During that first trip, they fell in love with the people of Ukraine, with their hospitality, and their genuine warm welcome. The two sisters returned to minister in Ukraine almost yearly. When they turned 18, they decided to move to Ukraine, and got involved with Noah's Ark within their first year. Samantha and Hope stayed with Irina's father, their host family, when they first arrived, and became familiar with all 12 of Irina's siblings!

At first, they were participants in the camps which were "very extreme" for them. Camping in tents, bathing in the river, no western comforts available... It was a hard transition. But they love it.

When asked about her impression of Noah's Ark, Samantha replied, "We absolutely love everything that Noah's Ark does. I'm amazed by how many ideas they come up with. They are always changing to meet the current needs. We've just so enjoyed and appreciated that it's not a formula ministry and that it evolves with the changing needs of the people they minister to. My sister and I have enjoyed being a part of the camps and the trips to Poland to get humanitarian aid. It has been inspiring to see how both Peter and Irina are so dedicated. [It] has given us a broader view of what ministry is, and their example has increased our willingness to give of our time and resources as well. Peter lives at the Ark, he lives the mission. His life has been convicting to me and made me want to do more.

"Working with them encourages me to be a better person and be a better Christian. When I got involved about nine years ago, I was more of a baby Christian. Irina changed my outlook on so many things in a good way. She's made me understand the true meaning of being hospitable. I've loved her view. She showed me what it means to not be judgmental towards people. She taught me that we're all the same; no person is better than another person. It's changed my outlook on everything.

"To be honest our friendship is not defined by age. I mean I'm 28 and she's in her 40s, but she's probably my closest friend. I've grown to appreciate her greatly. I can just see the way she truly loves God and people. I think the biggest way that my personal life has changed is by learning to see people through God's eyes. I guess you could say I learned how to truly love and serve people of all kinds. I've learned so many lessons from Irina."

One of the things that impresses everyone who knows Irina and Peter is how well they work with people of different denominations. They gather people from different churches for one purpose. And that purpose gets accomplished, whether it is sharing the gospel with children, ministering to families, or taking goods to those stranded without help because of the war. They unite under one cause: to minister to the people Jesus died for, bringing the Kingdom of God to earth.

So Many Others

These are only a fraction of the remarkable men and women who have touched so many lives through the Noah's Ark Mission. Hundreds of people have made Noah's Ark the success it is today, and volunteers and doners continue to make it possible for so many to not only hear the Good News of Jesus Christ, but to see to love of Christ in action. Peter and Irina are excellent ambassadors and true disciples of Christ. It would not be a bad thing to follow their example.

Some of the children who came to their home for Bible study later became helpers for the children's camp. All the volunteers have been very positive and seemed to maintain an optimistic and cheerful attitude no matter what circumstances, trials, and mishaps occurred. The camp leaders genuinely showed their love for the children who came to the Noah's Ark Camp. Receiving kind, thoughtful, patient, caring love and attention was a new experience for far too many of those children who attended the camps.

There are those who come to sort through the donated goods, package them, write notes, pray, mail packages, pack trucks, clean, cook, wash, decorate, set up tents, dig and plant, build, donate goods, plan camps, drive, plan and pray, and on it goes.

Peter recounted a story of how God goes before us to prepare the way. During the early stages of the ministry, Peter and Irina were gearing up for three summer camps. While Peter was busy readying the campsite, Irina went shopping for food and provisions for the first camp. Irina called Peter with the bad news that their money had all been spent and there were no more funds available to them. The prices of food fluctuated considerably at that time and there was no real way of knowing how far their money would go. This turbulent time tested their faith, causing moments of doubts.

Peter resolved to tackle the immediate challenge of the first camp, deferring other plans.

Meanwhile, in the United States, Al Yeatts visited the church office to collect a donation for his upcoming mission trip to Ukraine. There he encountered Andrew Romonov, who inquired about the mission. He asked Al if there was anything he could do for the mission.

Al jokingly replied, "Yah, give us $2,000!"

Upon hearing this Andrew sank to the floor, swiftly retrieved the sum from his wallet, and upon rising, he handed the cash to Al! All $2,000!

Although he knew the Tkachuks, he had never contributed to their mission before. Peter learned the rest of this story much later. Andrew had unexpectedly come into a substantial sum of money and deliberated about what to do with it. There were several things he *wanted* to do, including buying a newer car for his wife. He asked God if he could use this money for himself and was impressed with the answer that he could use all but $2,000. When he heard the exact amount that Al proposed in jest, he knew that God wanted him to give it toward the mission. When Al arrived in Kiev, he spotted Peter and waved excitedly, and with a huge smile told him that he had a great surprise for him!

Peter, relieved to hear about the funds, realized that now they didn't have to take a bus, which they called a taxi.

Life is good for the one who is generous and charitable, conducting affairs with honesty and truth. Their circumstances will never shake them, and others will never forget their example. They will not live in fear or dread of what may come, for their hearts are firm, ever secure in their faith. –Psalm 112:5-7 TPT

Chapter 7 - New Beginnings

Greater love has no one than this: to lay down one's life for one's friends. –John 15:13 NIV

The War Began

On February 24, 2022, Irina got a call from her husband in Ukraine at the camp. Russians had bombed Kyiv, Kharkiv, Odessa and Donbas, and the border posts with Russia and Belarus were attacked. She could hardly believe what she was hearing, but the news channels showed images of her native country under attack. Irina was planning on returning to Ukraine later that month, but upon hearing such news, she felt anxious to return immediately. Interestingly, Irina and her husband had just recently obtained their US citizenship and had US passports—a timely accident?

Irina got on the phone and quickly arranged to fly to Germany, where her sister lived. Peter and her son, Danial, were in Ukraine and her eldest daughter, Nadia, made her own plans to accompany her mom. After Irina and Nadia arrived, while anxious to be united with her husband, Irina felt strongly that she shouldn't enter Ukraine without bringing supplies. The four women: Irina, Nadia and Irina's sisters living in Germany, Maria and Olga, bought as many supplies as they could. They procured a truck, then tried to cross the border into Ukraine from Poland. At that point, the crossing was in chaos, and they couldn't get the supplies across. A big team from Germany unloaded the supplies and departed.

Irina and Nadia were stranded, with no way of transferring their aid across the border. They asked for help from as many people as possible who looked like they had some authority, policemen and soldiers, important looking men in suits, etc. But the Lord chose to use a 21-year-old woman.

"When she learned of our need, she found a truck and a driver willing to assist, and within hours they were at the border." Irina couldn't believe it. "Praise God," Irina cried, "for answering our prayers and sending help from the least expected places! We are seeing that our work is not done in vain, and we are praying for the strength to continue. May it bring glory to God and may God bless you (supporters) for being part of our team. We feel loved and supported knowing that so many of you are praying for us and the people of Ukraine."

Fortunately, Peter and Irina had a US passport and were able to cross the Ukrainian borders as the country had stopped all able-bodied men from leaving Ukraine. Irina continued to bring trucks with provisions from Germany to Ukraine while Peter, Danial, and a team member, Samantha joined her in Germany to help collect humanitarian aid and transport it to the border.

Crossing the border was no small feat. The border was chaos with inhumane conditions. There were many disabled, and small children traveling without parents. There was no consistent treatment, and there were long lines everywhere. There was also discrimination. The people they saw had no hope, and their eyes were filled with fear.

They prayed for God to send them the right people on their way to the border and the Lord provided answers to their prayers. They were given papers that allowed them to skip lines. Everyone was grateful for the work they were doing and eager to help them do it.

Their first truck of humanitarian aid entered Ukraine on March 3, 2022, first to Vinnytsia then to the Ark. Irina and Peter continued to organize and bring in supplies from Germany. They exhausted themselves but could not rest upon seeing the dire needs of so many people.

In the short time of one week, six loads of humanitarian aid had been collected and sent to Vinnytsia. It was distributed to churches hosting refugees, check points where civilians and soldiers guarded the entrance to Vinnytsia, and to the Ark.

Transformation

No one could imagine that what began as a children's ministry would be transformed within one day into a place of refuge. As people fled the war zones, the property that Peter, Irina, and the many volunteers had been remodeling became a place of rescue, safety and warmth. Before the government was able to organize and plan for the relocation of displaced citizens, Noah's Ark was ready with its doors open. The Tkachuks could never have imagined that the buildings would be used in this way; they were in awe when realized that this was God's plan all along.

The symbol of the Ark became a reality.

Refugees arrived at the camp by the hour. Some had a suitcase or a backpack, others had nothing. They were so glad to have a safe and warm place to sleep and a hot meal. The timing could not have been more perfect. The heat in the building had just been completed, so the people fleeing the bombings had a warm place to stay before they moved on. The whole emphasis of the Noah's Ark ministry immediately refocused on finding ways of helping their fellow citizens in this troubling time.

The Ark is in a village 45 minutes from Vinnytsia, away from the bombing and a distance from the fighting. A small team began living in the Ark, hosting about 35 refugees on average. The volunteers were up day and night, caring for the needs of the refugees and welcoming them at all hours. Some were there for a few days to gather their strength on the way to the border. Others stayed longer, remaining safe at the Ark until they could determine their next move. The team was glad to have the opportunity to share the love of Jesus Christ.

Irina writes in a letter dated 2-28-22:

Thank you so much for praying for me and all of Ukraine. I made it to Germany and as soon as I landed in Berlin, a lady called and offered to get me to the border with few supplies. That was my original plan when I arrived, I wanted to get to Ukraine as quickly as possible. After hearing about the current situation in Ukraine, I immediately knew it would not be right to go to Ukraine without gathering humanitarian aid. Stores are emptying out, pharmacies are closing, and many supplies are impossible to find. I have two sisters living in Germany. Together, we have been contacting every single person we know and raising up a team of people to help provide for the needs of my dear Ukrainian people. A lot of humanitarian aid has been donated, as well as an old van. It needs some mechanical work. And then we are hoping to be able to use it to bring food and supplies to the border. We will need to look for another option for transportation as this van is very old and unreliable, but it is what we have right now. Peter and Daniel are close to the Romanian border, along with a big team from Vinnytsia. They are going to meet us at the border to take food and supplies to the destinations in need. We are currently working with people that have connections to help get through the borders more quickly and easily, as the borders are complete chaos right now. The team on the Ukrainian side is also looking for a building to help host refugees and get them across the border. The lines are days long and the needs are endless.

In July of 2022, Peter and Irina were able to spend two weeks in Germany and Poland, visiting family and gathering humanitarian aid. They were able to spend a few days with Irina's family in Germany. Irina reports in her letter,

I can't even begin to describe the joy and the different emotions I experienced. Since the war started, my family has had to scatter all over the world. Exactly half of my brothers and sisters are currently in Germany, as well as my mom. While in Germany, we sent off one of my sisters and her family to Canada. We don't know when or if we will all be together again. We are learning to cherish every moment we have together. I'm so thankful for that time."

Irina explained the events that had taken place.

While in Germany, we were able to get some much-needed

wheelchairs and walkers to distribute. We then headed to Poland to get humanitarian aid. Our friends from Vinnytsia, Samantha and Sasha, met us there with our big van. We went to a city where our friends and ministry partners from Vinnitsa are currently living. They have been there the past few months and have made connections at the local church. They told the pastors about the work we were doing, and they decided they would like to help. They bought enough supplies to fill about 1/4 of our big bus! That was a big blessing!

It is always encouraging for us and those we visit abroad. Everyone is longing to go back home but understands that it might not be time yet. Please pray for wisdom and guidance for these families to know what to do. It's hard to be living in limbo.

After that, we headed to a city closer to the border and were able to buy other needed items to completely fill the van.

When the war started, we turned to prayer seeking guidance. Soon after, many people started contacting us sharing their urgent needs and telling us harrowing experiences. They remain in very dangerous cities which lack basic amenities and essential supplies. Thankfully, the postal service continues to work, and we started sending these families packages. We started sending about 30 to 50 packages per week, but now we're getting more than 300 requests per week and the numbers keep going up. We try to send off as many as possible, but we aren't always able to accommodate that many people.

In these packages, we have the most essential items. Food, laundry detergent, dish soap, personal hygiene items, a Bible and something sweet for each family. If there are kids in the family, we give a toy to each child. Other times, people have specific requests like blankets, towels, pillows, pots, pans et cetera. If we are able, we try to pack those items as well.

Each package weighs roughly 30 pounds and costs between $35 and $50, determined by the size of the recipient family. There are moments of concern, fearing it might be our final effort running out of aid, but God continues to supply. He has worked many miracles for us to keep going. We don't know how much longer we will be able to sustain this mission, but we will continue as God provides.

The work at the Ark continued, with several building projects and packing boxes sent by post to people who had contacted them and requested supplies. The finished part of the building became a storage facility and an assembly line for the many packages to be sent out. Supplies were replenished by shipping containers full of goods shipped from the US, and donations from Samaritan's Purse and the Mennonite church. These sources were able to provide the Ark with most of the food needed for the boxes, which enabled them to continue to minister in this way. They were able to help roughly 5,400 families with humanitarian aid boxes shipped all over Ukraine.

During this time, the Ark was buzzing with people and activity from Thursday to Saturday. There were friends and volunteers from various places at the Ark packing the boxes to ship on Sundays. Some days people came to help Irina reorganize the items. There were food, clothes, hygienic items, blankets, sleeping bags, flashlights, lanterns, candles, portable chargers, toys, candy and toys for children, and others. Every week volunteers took items out of the container and organized them in a logical way. When eager volunteers come, they found items quickly and efficiently filled the orders.

There is constant organization of all these stations. Often 20 to 40 people came to help. The people also needed to be fed, so the team spent a lot of time preparing meals. This became the women's weekly schedule. Many volunteers were unbelievers just wanting to do something tangible to help their countrymen. At times, the team invited children to help with the packages. These children came from nearby villages and picked out items for their fathers or for packaging for soldiers. When a child helped, their picture was taken and included in the boxes that were sent to their father. At times, the children drew pictures or wrote encouraging words to children or soldiers they had some connection with.

The team also worked with many government volunteers when they came to talk and rest, or to sleep. The team also fed them.

While it was mostly women doing this work, other volunteers helped Peter with the numerous construction projects. The Ark became a workshop.

The City of Kherson

As the war continued in Ukraine, God continued to open new doors for ministry. The Tkachuks were made aware of major needs in the city of Kherson and its surrounding region. Kherson[1] is a port city near the Black Sea, is divided by the Dnipro River. At this time one side of the river was under Ukrainian control and the other side of under Russian occupation. Kherson had been occupied by Russia for nine months—from initial invasion on February 24th until the fall of 2022. The city didn't have grocery stores, hospitals or a police force. The police came from Mikolaiv[2] in the morning and left at night. Kherson was heavily targeted and rarely a day went by without the area being bombed.

In May of 2023, the Tkachuks decided that they wanted to go see for themselves what the conditions were. When they arrived in Kherson, they realized they were not prepared for what they saw and felt. There was not a building standing that hadn't been affected. The stores and houses were either damaged or boarded up. They saw only a few resolute people in the street; 70% of the population had evacuated. It felt surreal for them to walk the quiet, deserted streets.

In line with their personal experience during their years of ministry, they saw God's light shining brightly in Kherson. Many people there were drawn to put their faith in God. The Tkachuks and those who traveled with them were able to locate a church service with 250 people in attendance. 90% of the attendees were not familiar with the gospel, nor had they been church attenders before the war. The Tkachuks and their team were given the opportunity to sing and share the message that the Kherson people were dearly loved, not only by God, but by others. By their presence, Peter and his team demonstrated that truth.

After leaving the church, they also visited three nearby villages. It was disheartening to see the destruction and distress of the people living there. Everyone they talked to had a story of a brother, son, father or other relative who had died, currently was, or had been a prisoner of war. One woman told us that her son had been a prisoner for three months. He normally weighed 210 pounds but came out of that experience weighing only 85 pounds. Another woman told us a story of how her husband was taken prisoner because the Russians had found a Ukrainian flag in their house. She reported that he had been tortured with electric shock for three months before they finally let him go, but by then he was no longer able to talk. He was slowly recovering and had started to speak a little again. These and other stories of tragedy and hardship deeply touched the hearts of the hearers.

Their visit to Kherson was under God's protection. Reportedly it had been the calmest day they had had in a long time. The day after the Tkachuks left there were 86 bombings in the city and directly within the region where they had been. God wanted these people to hear the message that Peter and Irina brought.

True to form, this was not just a fact-finding mission.

Shortly after this visit, they partnered with Pastor Serge of the church they had visited and promised their support. The Noah's Ark team learned that Pastor Serge had an opportunity to immigrate to the United States, urged on by his children living in the states, but he didn't go. Pastor Serge wanted to stay and share the gospel of Jesus Christ with as many people as possible.

He led the church through the nine months of the Russian occupation and only had to cancel church services *once*. He is (as of this writing) still fighting for the salvation of his countrymen as well as fighting stage four cancer. Pastor Serge's caring for the people in this area is essential. Those who lived through the Russian occupation struggle greatly and suffer with trauma and depression. They have lost their homes and their hope. Serge was determined that they have an opportunity to find healing and hope again through their relationship with Jesus Christ.

Peter and Irina and her children Danial, Anna and Nadia plus seven others made trips to this region monthly to bring in supplies and to support the courageous efforts of Serge. Peter and the team were disturbed by the number of elderly, disabled, and stranded people there. In July 2023, they planned to return to the area and bring a couple of contractors who could ascertain projects that could be completed. They wanted to give an estimate of the costs to repair some of the houses to make them livable. The Noah's Ark team hoped to help ten families by repairing at least one room in their home so they could occupy it safely. They also planned to provide them with essential supplies.

Early in June, Peter and the team visited a local dormitory where refugees from the eastern part of the country were living. They listened to stories of how the individuals were forced to leave their homes and everything they'd spent their lives building. As they listened during these visits, the reality (and insanity) of war settled in their hearts. Peter and the team were able to share the gospel and sing with them, answering questions about God and scripture. Everyone in attendance was encouraged by the team's visit.

The refugees expressed grief and longing to return to their old, familiar lives. One refugee from the Lugansk region echoed his longing with a heartfelt poem that laments what is now lost to him:

Oh, how I want to go home where the cherries are sweet, and the roses are beautiful!

Where grapes, strawberries, and plumbs grow.

Oh, how I want to go home to be with parents, friends, and acquaintances.

We have been scattered.

Oh, to see my favorite pond and familiar woods, to smell cherry trees!

Oh, how I want to go home, to walk in familiar places, my school, my college, the places where I became me.

The trauma of war, the loss of home and loved ones will impact Ukraine and its people for decades. Grief and trauma are best processed with others. Trauma isn't what happens to us, it's what happens *inside* us as we respond to what happens to us. The long-term effects of trauma diminish through grieving. Sharing with others meets the emotional needs of safety and love. The men's camps were a good place for this: a safe, loving environment to sort out their feelings and experiences with each other and to gain strength and hope from one another.

[1] "Kherson." *Encyclopædia Britannica*, Encyclopædia Britannica, inc., 15 Apr. 2024, www.britannica.com/place/Kherson-Ukraine.

[2] "Mykolayiv." *Encyclopædia Britannica*, Encyclopædia Britannica, inc., 28 Apr. 2024, www.britannica.com/place/Mykolayiv-Ukraine.

The Flood

On June 6, 2023, the Kakhovoka Dam[1] under Russia's military control, breached, and the city of Kherson was subsequently flooded. Providentially, Peter and his team were headed toward that area loaded with humanitarian aid and supplies to rebuild some houses. They were the first responders!

They could not imagine what they were going to face. When they arrived in Kherson, the smell overwhelmed them; it was something they were not ready for. They described it as a smell that was a mixture of marsh water, sewer water, and rotting carcasses. Everywhere they looked, they saw the aftermath of the flood. Any grass, plants, or trees that the water touched were now brown and lifeless.

They could not have imagined the condition of the houses, which were absolutely destroyed. Some houses had walls and ceilings made from a mixture of clay and hay; those structures were impossible to salvage. The water filled the houses to the roofs, destroying everything inside. The mud was so thick that almost everything in the houses had to be thrown away. But Peter and his team were able to pump water basements and wells in some homes. They helped carry out furniture and shoveled out mud in the homes they deemed salvageable. If there was anything to retrieve, they helped the residents bring items outside, hoping to save those items.

Unfortunately, many of the houses could only be condemned.

In some areas, the soil was so saturated that even after pumping the water out of a well or a basement, it just filled back in again. In addition, all the wells in the villages were contaminated, leaving most people without running water, gas or electricity. Peter's team brought in bottled water, clothes, propane tanks, food, and cleaning supplies to help. More than anything, what the Noah's Ark team brought was hope and love. Their very presence was life-giving and had lasting value.

Peter's team was able to partner with the local church in Kherson again, giving out 250 boxes of goods. Since the number was limited, the church came up with a system to give out tickets to the first 250 people. Other people started arriving throughout the night, even sleeping outside, to make sure that they would receive the supplies. Peter and the team were saddened that these people had to suffer so and deeply regretted that some had to be turned away. Once again, they were reminded of how important the Noah's Ark ministry was.

Meanwhile, the bombing in Kherson continued relentlessly. Hope seemed to have been swept away by the receding flood waters, leading the inhabitants helpless and afraid. Speaking with people who were hysterical with nowhere to go and realizing that there were hundreds of lives ruined was a life-altering experience. Seeing all the destruction was difficult to process. The team and the people of Kherson wept.

[1] "Kakhovka Reservoir." *Encyclopædia Britannica*, Encyclopædia Britannica, inc., www.britannica.com/place/Kakhovka-Reservoir. Accessed 7 May 2024.

Chapter 8: The Ark in High Seas

The Lord is my shepherd, I lack nothing. He makes me lie down in green pastures, he leads me beside quiet waters, he refreshes my soul. He guides me along the right paths for his namesake. Even though I walk through the darkest valley, I will fear no evil, for you are with me; Your rod and your staff, they comfort me. You prepare a table before me in the presence of my enemies. You anoint my head with oil, My cup overflows. Surely your goodness and love will follow me all the days of my life, and I will dwell in the house of the Lord forever. –Psalm 23:1-6 NIV

Women's and Children's Camp – July 2023

It was early in the morning in Ukraine at the women's camp. Women and children begin to stir from their tents distributed under the trees. Mothers and children giggled and whispered, wondering what the next few days would hold. The night had been filled with a show of thunder and lightning that had been thrilling to some. But it added to the fears of others and concerned the camp leaders.

Forty-two women—wives, children and mothers of fallen soldiers—responded to an invitation to escape from their lives overshadowed by fear, uncertainty, worry, and grief. As they stepped from the bus, a fresh realm welcomed them-one that was both recognizable and distant. The awareness of their nation being at war faded, and their hearts felt a peace that they hadn't felt for so long that it seemed unfamiliar.

The renovated schoolhouse was decorated with flowers, ribbons and strings of lights, and several round tables were decorated with tablecloths and vases of local wildflowers. The decorations sparked feelings of pride and love for their country. The newly built kitchen was already emitting the familiar smells of an upcoming meal. Those smells relieved the tension of seeing unfamiliar people.

This was the fruit of many people's labors. In early May, work was underway on the bathrooms and kitchen, making significant progress. The electricity in both buildings was successfully accomplished, prompting much rejoicing. However, as these two projects neared their end, another endeavor emerged. The Noah's Ark team decided to put up the large frame tent that had been donated. The tent was heavy-duty and required a foundation to be poured prior to setting it up.

Following much toil and sweat, the huge structure stood complete, and the volunteers successfully transferred the humanitarian aid provisions into the tent. With the building now available for camp activities, its readiness coincided perfectly with the upcoming summer women's camps. Truly, God's timing is perfect.

During the days leading up to camp, there were so many unknowns as the team anxiously awaited the arrival of participants. The intercession in prayer was for the camp and its attendees, as well as for the 100,000 refugees in Vinnytsia who fled the eastern war zone. Irina's parents had a good connection to the City Council, so she had access to various kinds of lists—like a list of women who became widowed because of war. They could invite women from that list to the Noah's Ark Women's Camp that July.

Because of some of the obstacles and tough situations they had to face, the team questioned if they were doing the right thing (even knowing the camps were God directed). Having had to face tough situations before, they knew they must not let fear and doubt make decisions for them, so, they pressed forward.

They were so grateful they did after seeing the fruit of their labors.

The territory for camp had to be prepped, and the volunteers found and gathered to the site. Everyone was doing their part as they anticipated ministering to the war-torn families. There were so many unknowns.

The team had never ministered to people experiencing trauma and grief of this extent before. They were concerned about how to minister to them. They didn't want to say the wrong things.

An answer to prayer arrived in the form of two women counselors from the US who had immigrated from Ukraine. They heard about the need for people who could help women experiencing trauma. These two women felt the call, took time from their work and families, and came to help. Their suggestions and guidance were greatly appreciated. Through the women's guidance, the team realized that people facing unimaginable pain don't need to hear pretty words, they needed *love*. Hurting people required someone who would listen and interact with them normally, notwithstanding the profound grief they were enduring.

After the women and children arrived Wednesday night, July 26, 2023, a terrible storm threatened their plans for camp. Peter and Irina gathered the volunteers and prayed together for guidance. As they worshipped God and declared their faith in Him, a huge weight lifted from their shoulders. They let Jesus carry their worries, receiving his renewed invitation to cast all their cares on Him.[1] Peter and Irina felt that peace that passes all understanding[2] and that peace remained throughout the days of the camp. The Noah's Ark team members were thankful also for the prayers of others during this time at camp, certain God had answered them.

Irina asked Peter to share something at the opening of the time at camp. He was unsure of what to say, but as he began to address the women before him, he felt an inspiration from God. After acknowledging that he did not and could not understand the depth of their grief, he told them that God could understand.

God could not bear the sight of his Son, Jesus, being hung on the cross to die a criminal's death. He darkened the sky and caused the earth to tremble. God knew their pain and could help them bear it. Jesus is described in Isaiah 53:3 as being a man of sorrow and well acquainted with grief. These women were pointed to God, because He could help them through, and those who looked to Him for help received it.

The variety of camp activities provided a space for joy, and for processing grief. The women painted flowers together, made macramé purses, exercised to music, danced silly dances, rode the zip line. They took a ride in a wagon pulled by a horse through the peaceful countryside and waded in the nearby stream. Some got massages. All of them came together after the evening meal for songs, a message and prayer.

The children had their own program filled with many games and activities. They got to be silly and carefree which was so needed. They too rode the zipline, the wagon, and visited the stream with their mothers.

Throughout the time in the camp, some of the wives and mothers of fallen soldiers shared their stories. Listeners felt the heavy cost of life the war had taken as the women shared about their loved ones. But now, the listeners could put names and faces to the statistics.

They could see Andrey, who had left behind his beautiful wife and three daughters with stunning blue eyes. They could see Sasha, who left behind his mother to care for his two children. They could see Max, who left behind his beautiful wife, Tanya, at the young age of 22. They could see Sveta, who was left caring for her seven children while her husband was held prisoner of war somewhere in Russia.

Statistics transformed into individuals with heartbreaking narratives and unimaginable suffering.

During their time in the camp, these women cried together and shared their grief. By the end of the camp experience, many found themselves laughing for the first time since their loved one was taken from them. At the close of their time at the camp, the ladies shared their testimonies:

"I have never felt so much love anywhere or from anyone."

"For the first time in months, I started sleeping through the night."

"You have given me hope for the future and a will to keep living."

"I initially decided to come to camp because of my kids. I now realize how much I needed this time and can't thank you enough for bring a bit of joy back into my life."

"You have helped me start the process of healing."

"God worked miracles at this camp," Irina reflected, "and we are so thankful for each person who helped make it possible. Please continue to pray for these sweet families. Pray that God would continue to surround them with His love as they learn how begin again with hope."

The second woman's retreat occurred a few weeks later—from August 16-20, 2023. The break between camps allowed the team a short time to recharge, reconnect with their families, reflect on the previous camp, and strategize for the upcoming one.

This time, the women arrived at the camp by a bus transported by a friendly volunteer. Women of different ages and backgrounds came with excitement and anticipation, daring to anticipate joy despite the hardship they had been enduring. During the check-in process, they received directions to their designated tents, settling in comfortably. The evening meal was only a taste of the joy and fellowship they would be sharing for the next few days.

The women felt welcomed by tables set and adorned with charming vases of local flowers. The cooks prepared delicious food, and a team of loving hands served it with smiling faces. The women were treated like special guests at a celebrity function and felt truly acknowledged and valued.

After dinner, music filled the air, accompanied by a warm welcome speech and introductions to the volunteers. Each person felt God's presence, as if they were being enveloped in a divine embrace. Throughout the week, these comforting moments of connection were provided by both the Noah's Ark team and their fellow participants.

In this unified support, the camp attendees found healing for their emotional wounds, solace for their grief, and a renewed sense of hope for the days to come. The love that encircled them became a wellspring of encouragement for every woman present. even the volunteers received the reward of joy that comes with ministering to others. They too suffered the trauma that comes with war and uncertainty. As they served the other women, as they cried with them and laughed with them, God brought healing to their own hearts.

Men helping with the children, children, women participants, women volunteers—all experienced peace in the middle of a storm, a peace passing all understanding. They tasted the goodness of God, and their hearts were glad.

Irina explained, "Many years ago, we started doing camps and different retreats. We held retreats for men, women, and families. But when the war started, we felt that it was not appropriate to hold camps where people would come as they did before with the expectations to relax, have a good time of fellowship, spend time with God, and get away from daily responsibilities. We understood that we are also responsible for what is happening in our country, and we wanted to do our part."

One woman camper revealed her mindset coming into the camp experience, "I did not want any kind of vacation, no restarts. I did not understand how I could be in a different location and not think about my son, how could I think differently? I did not understand the word 'restart.'"

Another testimony said, "I have thought about how to name it. It is a camp, retreat, a place for restoration. A place where we can work through our pain that everyone is experiencing together. These five days flew by so fast. They were full of kindness, compassion, and love. These days were very remarkable for us."

One of the workers said, "We have cried here, but we have also experienced joy. Sometimes in order to feel joy, you need to let the tears out. It is such a delight when we can be vulnerable with one another."

Another participant evaluated her experience and said, "I am very pleased with how professional everything was organized–and from the heart. Every detail in every moment impressed me. The combination of the wonderful nature and the generosity and the kindness of the people who did all of this. It was just the greatest atmosphere where the person felt free and comfortable."

"There was not a single day that I was here that I didn't have something to do. There was a lot of conversation and fellowship. There were a lot of ideas that allowed every one of us to learn something new in the master classes. We worked with our hands, we knitted, we created amazing, beautiful bouquets, we painted, we exercised," commented an enthusiastic camper.

"On the second day, the children started saying that they didn't want to leave," recalled a children's worker. "They said, 'We think that we're going to cry when we have to leave.' I was so surprised, I thought to myself, *I'm not doing anything to cause this change of heart.*"

The children thanked the team for not forcing them to do anything, and the team witnessed how just loving the children transformed them. Workers provided care and activities from 9:00

AM to 10:00 PM, a very demanding task which they performed with patience and always showing kindness.

One teenage boy shared that his tears flowed because he had never had a friend in his life; he was always alone. This was the only place that he had ever found a friend. He had to leave the camp, but he would leave with the realization that he could have friends and wouldn't be alone anymore.

A childcare worker commented, "For me, this was encouraging, I realized that we are here for a reason. We need to listen to God and follow Him even when we don't see. This was a huge encouragement to me. On the final day, as we began bidding farewell to the children, it was surprising to witness those who had initially cried and resisted our company were the ones who ran to us offering hugs and inviting us for future visits. Tears flowed as some insisted that they weren't bidding farewell, but rather expressing a firm belief that they would meet again. I was heartened that the Noah's Ark leadership had already planned a future meeting with the children and was planning to keep in touch with them going forward."

The volunteers heard many words of hope from the women:

"I started wanting to live..."

"I saw a new goal for my life..."

"I was renewed..."

"I am stronger..."

"I saw those who were walking beside me were like me; I am not alone..."

"I received such incredible support, and I was so happy to be here these few days. I don't even want to leave. I was filled with so much kindness and genuine love that I was able to feel happiness, I was able to smile. I didn't know how much I needed that."

One of the counselors that traveled from the US to help with these camps reflected on her process. "We all feel the war," she said. "We all think that we understand, at least a little, the people who have lost someone. But now I realize that we do not understand even 5% of what they are going through. Before the camp, there was some doubt with our team about whether we could handle it. We wondered if we could be of any help. And most importantly, where do we find a team of people who could love well? I understood that a person who has experienced trauma does not always act in pleasant, cooperative ways. That was my fear. But one day when I was reading the Bible, God showed me through his word what his desire was for the church: to care for orphans and widows."[3]

She continued, "Coming here, I led part of the program. I opened with a topic for discussion during a group session. Maybe the losses in their lives were something they were trying to avoid talking about or thinking about. The importance of all this is hard to explain in words. But just imagine, through this traumatizing event, this person is left alone to cope by themselves. In most cases that I personally know, family members turn away, and friends don't know what to say. But here, during these camps, women become friends with other women who are facing similar challenges. I came here to listen to and to help the women who attended camp. I wanted to make sure that they would have someone to understand them and to help them process, someone who could share in their pain and to share in their joy.

"It was such a joy to witness how in the period of just a few days, perspectives were changed. The eyes are the mirror to the soul. People can say everything is okay when asked, that everything is super, but the eyes tell the truth. When the women come on the first day to these retreats, their eyes expressed their doubts and fears. The women were closed and cautious. But by the last day, everything had changed! We hugged and cried out of happiness. The women's eyes were filled with joy and sparkled with hope! The women come here filled with agony, they were in various stages of the grieving process over a lost loved one. But there is such an interesting phenomenon that happens when people come together and share their pain. When people come together, and process their experiences, pain on pain produces joy. We received such delight in each other. We not only became acquaintances, but we also became friends, like sisters. Who can understand your situation better than the one who has experienced a similar situation? From such a person you can receive advice that will help you cope. When you fall, you can ask advice from this person. It was such a treasure to experience such unity with one another. I am certain that God will not abandon these people. This time away has made me search my heart and to ask myself, 'I am ready to be obedient and partner with Jesus?'"

Irina reflected on the 2023 women's camps and said, "We understand that God prepared this place and time for these women. Throughout the entire camp, God showed us so many miracles and affirmed that this was what He wanted. The desire of my heart is to continue. I want to continue working with these families and individuals and help them in any way I can." Then she challenged us all with these words, "I don't know about you, but I think, as people, we all have doubts. We all have worries, and we think that we won't be able to do things that come to our mind. We think that maybe this was not God's idea, or that this is not the time, or that we are not equipped to carry out the plan. We excuse ourselves from even starting what we believe God wants us to do by thinking of all the things we don't have, all the reasons it won't work, and all the ways we aren't qualified or equipped.

"But I want to encourage you, if you take the first step, God will take care of the rest. He will provide finances and the people that will help you. Just pray for God to open your heart and give you confidence. So, if you have a thought, a dream, an idea about what you can do to expand the Kingdom of God, if you desire to share the love and hope, the freedom and joy that you enjoy with others, if you have ideas of ways to care for the practical needs of a person–don't be afraid-take the first step! God will meet you! It is God's desire that we love and serve one another. He will be with you, and Jesus will be your partner! Remember, we walk by faith, not by sight!"[4]

See YouTube: Noah's Ark, Retreat for wives and mothers of fallen soldiers https://youtu.be/LM-DIs4jUEM?si=ki-98ylHfFU7RA4-

The third camp in the summer of 2023 was for the families of fallen soldiers. The program was very similar to that of the women's camps. Irina writes in her newsletter:

Although it was an incredibly emotional camp, God used our team to love and support these precious people. We cried together and laughed together. We are thankful for each participant who joined us. We know that this was not an easy decision to make, but we are thankful that they trusted us. We are so thankful for God's provision of people, funds, and resources to make this camp possible. We stand in awe of what God can do! Please continue to pray for these sweet families pray that God would continue to surround them with his love."

Women were full of praise after the camp, saying things like:

"Thank you so much, I already miss you! I send you, my hugs! You guys are awesome! I've been rebooted!"

"We are glad we were able to spend time with you and have a chance to recover."

"You have totally recharged me and just and have inspired me to be creative!"

The comments, smiles and hugs are an encouragement to Irina and the team. They give the team members strength to continue. Thinking, "It was worth it!" echoing the words of Paul from Romans 8:18 (TPT):

I am convinced that any suffering we endure is less than nothing compared to the magnitude of glory that is about to be unveiled within us."

[1] 1 Peter 5:7

[2] Philippians 4:7

[3] James 1:27

[4] 1 Corinthians 5:7

Christmas Encounter 2023

Along with the relentless receiving, organizing, boxing up and delivering packages, the Ark team made plans to celebrate Christmas with three different groups:

1. Soldiers who were on leave, wounded soldiers, and chaplains.
2. Widows and family members of fallen soldiers.
3. Family members of soldiers who are still currently fighting and volunteers.

Over the course of a month, their team worked to create a Christmas wonderland at the Ark, then they celebrated Jesus's birth with nearly 1,000 people–three groups in three days. They planned every day for weeks prior to the encounter. They were unsure of how to minister to those who have suffered so much for their country. The team wanted to show God's love to those who have lost so much, seen so much, and hurt so much. They couldn't just say, "God loves you." It would not be understood or received. So, they had to show them.

Many people came to help transform the Ark into a wonderland. The location was decorated with thousands of colorful lights.

"We had a 'food street' where people could come and eat a big variety of tasty foods. We had chicken wings, hot dogs, soup, rice with meat, quesadillas, cotton candy, popcorn, pancakes, potato wedges, hot chocolate, a chocolate fountain, and other sweets and drinks. Of course, it was all free for the participants, and it was such a fun atmosphere for people to walk from tent to tent, ordering different food. We had great fellowship with one another! It is always encouraging for people to get together with others who are experiencing similar struggles." Irina reports with joy. "People were in awe when they arrived. They stepped into another world! We also invited a team of 40 highly sought-after professionals to perform a Musical Christmas Pageant. They were able to present the complete gospel."

Through their show, we remembered the true reason we celebrate Christmas—the birth of our savior, Jesus Christ! There were many laughs and tears shed during the show, which was done with such excellence. It was quite an amazing experience as the hearts responded. Everyone had the chance to answer the invitation to join Him at the table of grace. To those who responded, Jesus reconciled them to God, And God rescued them from the tyrannical rule of darkness, translating them into the kingdom ream of His beloved Son. For in the Son all our sins are canceled, and we have the release of redemption through his very blood."[1]

The first night, nearly 200 wounded soldiers and other military personnel arrived on eight buses. For them to come, permission had to be granted at the highest levels in Kiev, and defense systems had to be placed around the area of the Ark. Several of the men were healing from amputated limbs. Many of these men had recently returned from the frontlines with very serious injuries and had been in rehabilitation. Some were waiting for their limbs to heal before receiving prosthesis. Because of security, the soldiers were not told exactly where they were going.

They couldn't believe their eyes when they saw all the decorations, provisions and lights!

After spending so much time in the hospital and in recovery, they felt like they were whole again. Peter reported, "As you can imagine, it was a bit scary for us to invite this specific group of people. Our campsite was not completely ready and able to host people in wheelchairs or on crutches. Through the fear and many unknowns, God's providence and hand was seen in every detail. The preparations and accommodations for wheelchair access was completed the day before the soldier's arrival!"

The day these soldiers arrived was a miracle day, a day of God's favor. That day was the warmest day of the year with no rain, snow or wind. It reminded them of spring, and spring is a reminder of the newness of life. That day no warning sirens went off. If it had, the soldiers would have had to leave immediately. The peace and the love of God was tangible that day.

Peter echoes the words of Paul from Romans 8:18 when he said, "I am convinced that any suffering we endure is less than nothing compared to the magnitude of glory that is about to be unveiled within us" (TPT).

All the camp helpers' fears and doubts of being able to help these men vanished and everyone had a wonderful night together. Some soldiers rejoiced in the fact that this was the first time they laughed in months. Some rejoiced in that they felt hope again. The camp leaders were encouraged, and their faith was strengthened once again.

Family members of those serving in the military, family members of fallen soldiers, and refugees arrived the second and third night. When they arrived, they experienced the same display of lights and the food walk. It was exciting for the team to see many of the ladies and children who were in the summer camps. Many attendees said that the Noah's Ark campsite was like heaven on earth and that it had become their happy place.

So many people helped with the summer camps in 2023, providing 70% of the funds needed for the camps. There has been lasting fruit from these camps. Four ladies who attended camp are now regularly attending church and one has been baptized.

Irina reflected on her experiences through years of ministering. "I enjoy the daily fellowship with God and the peace and joy He provides, Irina confessed, "but my greatest joy is when God calls me out onto the water." Irina's faith makes walking on water as surefooted as walking on the earth. She asked to share one more miracle.

Peter and Irina came to the US for a short sabbatical. Peter thought out loud that it would be nice if the road into the camp were paved, especially if they were to host the wounded soldiers again. The five-mile dirt road into the camp was bumpy and full of potholes, which was not an easy ride for wounded soldiers still healing. While Irina was in Texas with some of her family, she got a call from Pastor Serge in Ukraine. He mentioned that several of the landowners nearby had heard about their camp and wanted to meet them. Irina conveyed that Peter would like to see the road paved to the Ark, and maybe, after meeting the farmers upon their return, they could ask them about it.

On her flight back to Sacramento, Irina got another call from Serge. He was excited to transmit that after his meeting with the landowners about other matters, without being prompted, they brought up the idea of paving the road into the Ark!

Their favor the God and man grows.

The mission and the miracles of Noah's Ark Ukraine are continually impacting the region around the Ark. Government officials are working with this mission as well. People from all around the area have been inspired to volunteer to help, coming daily for various reasons. Like a true ark, they are taken in and provided for. Numerous people want to help, so they sort and package goods to be mailed to families in need. Children come with their parents and draw pictures and write notes to the soldiers. Some come to feel the atmosphere of peace. Some are drawn to the hope seeming to reside there permanently. Some come to remember how to laugh. God's presence is all around them.

Peter talked about how the people of Ukraine have changed. Many left in fear at the beginning of the war, some now send money to help, but those who stayed have been united. They have become deaf to the sirens warning of incoming missiles and continue going about their business. The "If I live, I live. If I die, I die." attitude prevails. Many who remain in Ukraine refuse to live in fear. They have a determination that wasn't there before, a vision to work toward. They see a future for their children to, a free Ukraine, a united Ukraine.

No longer do they only think about themselves, a unifying compassion has been awakened within Ukraine. They no longer live for themselves, but for those who are hurting and in need. They not only look for outside help but are determined to provide help themselves. Even as Peter rejoices over the changes he sees in the people of Ukraine, he laments over the tremendous cost.

When I asked Peter what God was talking to him about these days, Peter responded, "Don't leave my people," the Lord told him. "Stay. Be with them during this hard time."

Peter understands that God wants him to bring people His comfort, to sit with them, put his arms around the traumatized in silence and introduce them to God's Kingdom. "It's what Jesus did, he stayed with us. He fed us and gave us hope. He talked about God's Kingdom. He promised a future and a hope." Peter also invites others into the work of expanding God's Kingdom, "There is a time for study, a time for practice, and after, a time to get to work."

Peter and Irina also realize that they must continually seek guidance from the Lord. If not, they will lose their way. The stories in this book tell of the amazing dedication and work that Peter and Irina do to spread the Kingdom of God. One might be seduced into thinking that God will be pleased with a person if they do enough works, but God's ways are not like our ways. God looks at the heart. A personal relationship with Jesus Christ starts in the heart through faith in Him. As love grows, works flow. But it must grow out from a grateful heart.

For God, the Faithful One, is not unfair. How can he forget the work you have done for Him? He remembers the love you demonstrate as you continually serve his beloved ones for the glory of his name.

–Hebrews 6:10 TPT

Peter and Irina continue as they started, seeing needs around them, asking God how they can make a difference, then acting in obedience out of a heart of worship.

As of this writing, the end of the war with Russia is not seen on the horizon, but the Tkachuks have a higher calling, a mandate to seek and save. The nation of Israel faced enemies too strong for them many times, but God delivered them. Perhaps that will be the future of Ukraine. "Some trust in chariots and some in horses, but we trust in the name of the Lord our God."[2]

Whatever the future of Ukraine, the future of Peter and Irina is secure.

[1] Colossians 1:12-13

[2] Psalm 20:7

Mission Statement of Noah's Ark Missions, Ukraine

Noah's Ark Missions exists to glorify God by loving and caring for people. We share the hope of the gospel of Jesus Christ with the lost, encourage the Saints, and come alongside the broken and suffering, so that they do not have to suffer alone. We strive to show people what it means to have a personal relationship with Jesus Christ; God is not only our savior, but he is also our father and friend who desires a close relationship with us as we go to him with our daily praises and struggles.

Information about and donations to Noah's Ark Ukraine missions can be sent through www.noahsarkmissions.com

Facebook, Instagram, and YouTube links are on their website.

https://www.facebook.com/noahsarkukrainemissions

https://www.instagram.com/n.o.a.h.s.ark/

https://www.youtube.com/@noahsark5449

https://www.noahsarkmissions.com/give/

Website Resources

"Crimean Peninsula." *Encyclopædia Britannica*, Encyclopædia Britannica, inc., 14 Feb. 2024, www.britannica.com/place/Crimean-Peninsula.

Education.com. "Trust Walk: Activity." *Activity | Education.Com*, 25 July 2012, www.education.com/activity/article/trust-walk/.

The Encyclopædia Brittanica Editors. "Kakhovka Reservoir." *Encyclopædia Britannica*, Encyclopædia Britannica, inc., 30 Apr. 2024, www.britannica.com/place/Kakhovka-Reservoir.

"Family-Based Immigrant Visas and Sponsoring a Relative." *USAGov*, www.usa.gov/sponsor-family-member. Accessed 27 Apr. 2024.

"Great Purge." *Encyclopædia Britannica*, Encyclopædia Britannica, inc., 6 Mar. 2024, www.britannica.com/event/Great-Purge.

"Holodomor." *Encyclopædia Britannica*, Encyclopædia Britannica, inc., 29 Mar. 2024, www.britannica.com/event/Holodomor.

"The Jesus Film | English | Official Full Movie HD." *YouTube*, Jesus Film Project, 9 Mar. 2020, www.youtube.com/watch?v=-Td05XH0TDg.

"Kakhovka Reservoir." *Encyclopædia Britannica*, Encyclopædia Britannica, inc., www.britannica.com/place/Kakhovka-Reservoir. Accessed 7 May 2024.

"Kherson." *Encyclopædia Britannica*, Encyclopædia Britannica, inc., 15 Apr. 2024, www.britannica.com/place/Kherson-Ukraine.

"The Life of George Muller." *GeorgeMuller.Org*, www.georgemuller.org/devotional/the-life-of-george-muller. Accessed 7 May 2024.

"Mykolayiv." *Encyclopædia Britannica*, Encyclopædia Britannica, inc., 28 Apr. 2024, www.britannica.com/place/Mykolayiv-Ukraine.

"Noah's Ark Ukraine Missions." *YouTube*, 27 Jan. 2022, youtu.be/K-CBBCweVac.

"The Prayer Walk." C.S. *Lewis Institute*, 8 June 2022, www.cslewisinstitute.org/resources/the-prayer-walk/.

Stevens, Patsy. "The Life of George Muller." *GeorgeMuller.Org*, www.georgemuller.org/devotional/the-life-of-george-muller. Accessed 5 May 2024.

"Zaporizhzhya." *Encyclopædia Britannica*, Encyclopædia Britannica, inc., 15 Apr. 2024, www.britannica.com/place/Zaporizhzhya-Ukraine.

"Crimean Peninsula." *Encyclopædia Britannica*, Encyclopædia Britannica, inc., 14 Feb. 2024, www.britannica.com/place/Crimean-Peninsula.

Education.com. "Trust Walk: Activity." *Activity | Education.Com*, 25 July 2012, www.education.com/activity/article/trust-walk/.

The Encyclopædia Brittanica Editors. "Kakhovka Reservoir." *Encyclopædia Britannica*, Encyclopædia Britannica, inc., 30 Apr. 2024, www.britannica.com/place/Kakhovka-Reservoir.

"Family-Based Immigrant Visas and Sponsoring a Relative." USAGov, www.usa.gov/sponsor-family-member. Accessed 27 Apr. 2024.

"Great Purge." *Encyclopædia Britannica*, Encyclopædia Britannica, inc., 6 Mar. 2024, www.britannica.com/event/Great-Purge.

"Holodomor." *Encyclopædia Britannica*, Encyclopædia Britannica, inc., 29 Mar. 2024, www.britannica.com/event/Holodomor.

"The Jesus Film | English | Official Full Movie HD." *YouTube*, Jesus Film Project, 9 Mar. 2020, www.youtube.com/watch?v=-Td05XH0TDg.

"Kakhovka Reservoir." *Encyclopædia Britannica*, Encyclopædia Britannica, inc., www.britannica.com/place/Kakhovka-Reservoir. Accessed 7 May 2024.

"Kherson." *Encyclopædia Britannica*, Encyclopædia Britannica, inc., 15 Apr. 2024, www.britannica.com/place/Kherson-Ukraine.

"The Life of George Muller." *GeorgeMuller.Org*, www.georgemuller.org/devotional/the-life-of-george-muller. Accessed 7 May 2024.

"Mykolayiv." *Encyclopædia Britannica*, Encyclopædia Britannica, inc., 28 Apr. 2024, www.britannica.com/place/Mykolayiv-Ukraine.

"Noah's Ark Ukraine Missions." *YouTube*, 27 Jan. 2022, youtu.be/K-CBBCweVac.

"The Prayer Walk." C.S. *Lewis Institute*, 8 June 2022, www.cslewisinstitute.org/resources/the-prayer-walk/.

Stevens, Patsy. "The Life of George Muller." *GeorgeMuller.Org*, www.georgemuller.org/devotional/the-life-of-george-muller. Accessed 5 May 2024.

"Zaporizhzhya." *Encyclopædia Britannica*, Encyclopædia Britannica, inc., 15 Apr. 2024, www.britannica.com/place/Zaporizhzhya-Ukraine.

Thank You

As we remember all that God has done and is doing through Noah's Ark Ministries, a simple "thank you" seems so inadequate. When we started this ministry back in the early 2000's, we started with nothing. To this day, as we plan different outreaches and continue building our campsite, we are constantly dependent upon the Lord for His provision in every aspect. He has been so faithful to provide for His work. We want to especially thank our home church, Arcade Baptist Church. God has used so many people along this journey and we have seen how the Lord has cared for us and blessed this ministry through His Church. One thing has been made so evident, this ministry is not our own. Noah's Ark is made up of hundreds of people around the globe who have a passion and desire for the work God is doing in Ukraine. Thank you to every single one of you who has played a role in this ministry, no matter how big or small. May the Lord be glorified and may His name be lifted high because of this ministry. We consider it a privilege and joy to be His hands and feet in a hurting world. Thank you to all who have joined us in following God's calling as we strive to share the greatest news of all, the Gospel of Jesus Christ. -Peter & Irina Tkachuk

I would like to extend my thanks to the Noah's Ark Board members who were so encouraging to me, to my brother who is so generous, who believes in me and who helped me organize my files.

Thanks to Peter and Irina for showing me what it looks like to be totally surrendered to Christ.

Thanks to my editor from Speak Fire Publishing, and my publisher and friend, Desiree Young and King's Glory Publishing House. You operate with a spirit of excellence.

I give thanks to the music of Wayne Shorter who gave me just the right vibe to write to.

I thank God who prompted me to and enabled me to accomplish the writing of this book.

I thank you dear readers for reading this book. -Lura Hunter

A Note & Gift from the Author

Thank you for taking the time to read my book. If this story has inspired or otherwise encouraged you, please leave a review. The more reviews I get, the more Amazon recommends my book. The more Amazon recommends my book, the more people get impacted by the story. You can find the link to leave a review here: **https://a.co/d/0ftruP1h**

If you grabbed the ebook, I encourage you to grab the paperback version: **https://a.co/d/0ftruP1h**

Lastly, I have a free gift as a thank you for purchasing my book and leaving a review: **https://kingsglorypublishi.wixsite.com/lurahunterfreegift**

About the Author

Lura Hunter is an author, missionary, and heart healer. She holds a master's in counseling and special education. She has worked as a speech therapist on the junior high and high school level for several years. While in the education field she also taught both students and teachers to write. Writing is something that Lura has always loved. She found it as her safe haven when trying to make sense of her own mental health. It was also her secret place with the Lord as she journaled about scriptures she studied. Today her writing takes a new form as she publishes her first book, *The Ark of Ukraine*. Lura has a passion for the lost. Her desire is not just to see them saved but to make disciples as the Great Commission commands. Lura has traveled to nine different countries: Brazil, Ghana, China, El Salvador, Ukraine, Cameroon, Papa New Guinea, Uruguay, and Indonesia. With each country she met new people and experienced God's heart in a new way.

When she is not on the mission field abroad, Lura takes on the role of healer for many. With over ten years of experience doing inner healing with Family Church, Lura currently serves as an intern with Exousia Ministries. There she helps people break out the things that keep them bound (I.e. generational curses, guilt, shame, anxiety, etc.) and helps them step into spiritual freedom by Sozo and Prophetic Heart Healing. She offers 1:1 Holy Spirit guided sessions to those who are searching for a way to break free once and for all and start living an abundant life. To book a session or to get more information, please visit her website at **https://www.lurahunter.com/**

Map of Ukraine

www.ingramcontent.com/pod-product-compliance
Lightning Source LLC
Chambersburg PA
CBHW070713130626
46553CB00005B/1973